American Route 66

American Route 66

Home on the Road

Photographs and Text by Jane Bernard and Polly Brown
With a Foreword by Michael Wallis

Museum of New Mexico Press   Santa Fe

Frontis: Boots Motel, Carthage. Missouri. Photo by Jane Bernard

Project editor: Mary Wachs
Design and production: David Skolkin
Map: Deborah Reade
Composition: Set in Stempel Garamond with Helvetica display.
Manufactured in Singapore
10 9 8 7 6 5 4 3 2 1

Library of Congress Cataloging-in-Publication Data
Bernard, Jane, 1961-
  American Route 66 : home on the road / by Jane Bernard and Polly Brown; foreword by Michael Wallis.— 1st ed.
  p. cm.
  ISBN 0-89013-459-6 (CB : alk. paper) — ISBN 0-89013-461-8 (PB : alk.paper)
  1. West (U.S.)—Description and travel. 2. United States Highway 66. 3. West (U.S.)—Biography. 4. Interviews—West (U.S.) 5. Oral history. 6. United States Highway 66—Pictorial works. 7. West(U.S.)—Pictorial works. 8. Historic sites—West (U.S.)—Pictorial works. I. Brown, Polly. II. Title.
  F595.3.B47 2003
  977—dc21
                                                                    2003006153

MUSEUM OF NEW MEXICO PRESS
Post Office Box 2087
Santa Fe, New Mexico 87504

Contents

ROUTE 66 IS A MAGICAL ROAD. It is arguably the most famous highway in the world. To countless travelers, a journey along this historic path of concrete and asphalt, which stretches across two-thirds of the continent, is as comforting and familiar as a visit to Grandma's house. Some have memories of the road that are bittersweet while still others harbor lingering images of overheated radiators, ice storms, bloody wrecks, and speed traps. But no matter what the mention of Route 66 brings to mind, no veteran of "the Mother Road" can say that this highway is in any way ordinary.

Route 66 is forever reinventing itself. Never static, always fluid and elastic, it remains a road of movement and change. Businesses open and close, highway landmarks appear and then vanish. Heroes and heroines of the road come and go. Retirement, death, and bad times take their toll. Change is both inevitable and necessary. Change offers challenges. Change keeps the road alive and well.

The wisest of those people who care about the historic importance and preservation of Route 66 realize this worn ribbon of highway is truly a linear village that winds out of Chicago and touches eight states — Illinois, Missouri, Kansas, Oklahoma, Texas, New Mexico, Arizona, and California — before it ends in Santa Monica. They understand it is important that the "village" of Route 66 remain as intact as possible without harming those individual characteristics that give each city, town, and attraction its unique place in the overall scheme of things. This necklace of enticements — natural and fabricated alike — must be protected or else, like a string of pearls that breaks, the entire necklace will fall apart.

Fortunately, more and more people realize that it is imperative that everyone work together toward the common goal of preservation. They understand that what is good for

Foreword

the old road in Missouri is good for the highway in New Mexico. Whatever helps boost Dwight, Illinois, boosts Holbrook, Arizona, as well.

To fully appreciate the attraction of Route 66, it is helpful to understand that the old road has endured several eras of history. Each of these periods has left an indelible impression on the people living and working along the road as well as on those travelers who still prefer to use its well-worn lanes.

Those new to this historic road must revisit each of the highway's eras in order to fully understand it. This is not hard to do because literature, film, photography, music, and art have each chronicled in detail the story of the fabled highway.

Begin the journey in the "Roaring Twenties," when the nation was between wars and on the wagon. Route 66 was created in 1926 and soon was on almost everyone's map.

Then came the turbulent 1930s, when tens of thousands of migrants fled the Great Depression and the Dust Bowl. Flocks of disenfranchised people packed up their few belongings and poured onto Route 66. The highway was clogged with Okies and other sad refugees escaping poverty and black clouds of choking dust. They followed the scent of orange blossoms, hoping to build new lives and piece together shattered dreams in California. Route 66 became known as "the Mother Road," a name coined by John Steinbeck in his acclaimed 1939 novel *The Grapes of Wrath*.

During World War II, the highway once more paid its dues. Civilians had little or no gasoline and few tires, automobile manufacturing was geared to the war effort, and Route 66 was filled with troop convoys. Uniformed hitchhikers were scattered up and down the road. General George S. Patton trained his desert warriors in the scorching Mojave Desert

8

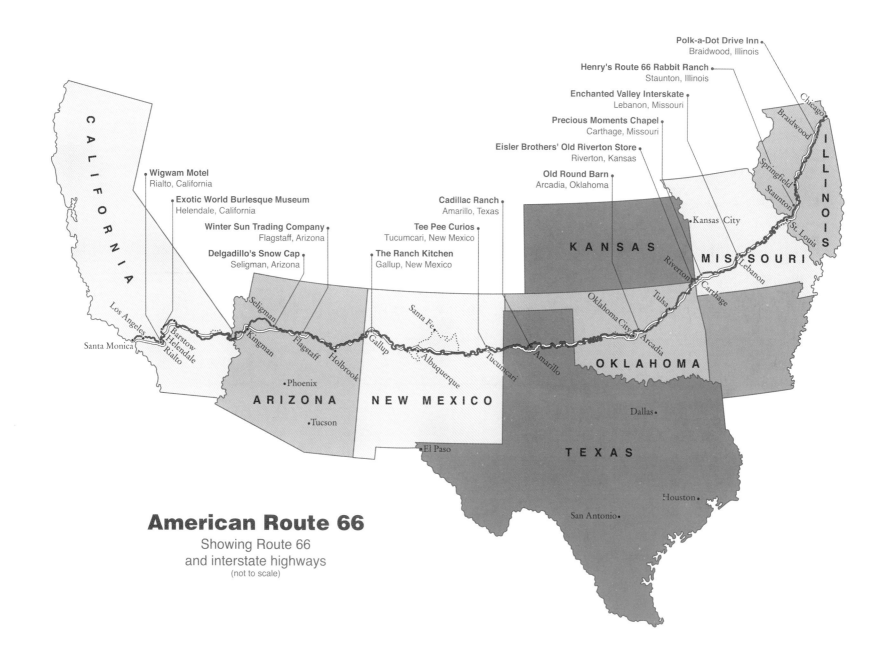

American Route 66
Showing Route 66
and interstate highways
(not to scale)

Polk-a-Dot Drive Inn
Braidwood, Illinois

Henry's Route 66 Rabbit Ranch
Staunton, Illinois

Enchanted Valley Interskate
Lebanon, Missouri

Precious Moments Chapel
Carthage, Missouri

Eisler Brothers' Old Riverton Store
Riverton, Kansas

Old Round Barn
Arcadia, Oklahoma

Cadillac Ranch
Amarillo, Texas

Tee Pee Curios
Tucumcari, New Mexico

The Ranch Kitchen
Gallup, New Mexico

Wigwam Motel
Rialto, California

Exotic World Burlesque Museum
Helendale, California

Winter Sun Trading Company
Flagstaff, Arizona

Delgadillo's Snow Cap
Seligman, Arizona

CALIFORNIA
ARIZONA
NEW MEXICO
KANSAS
MISSOURI
ILLINOIS
OKLAHOMA
TEXAS

Chicago
Braidwood
Springfield
Staunton
St. Louis
Kansas City
Riverton
Carthage
Lebanon
Tulsa
Oklahoma City
Arcadia
Santa Fe
Amarillo
Albuquerque
Tucumcari
Gallup
Holbrook
Flagstaff
Seligman
Kingman
Barstow
Helendale
Rialto
Los Angeles
Santa Monica
Phoenix
Tucson
El Paso
Dallas
Houston
San Antonio

not far from Route 66, and many of the captured German and Italian troops ended up in prison camps along the highway.

Route 66 experienced its glory years after the end of the war. The nation's postwar economy boomed. GIs returning home wanted to show their loved ones where they had trained, so they turned to Route 66. More automobiles were produced and greater numbers of people took to the road. They traveled east and west, visiting cities and tourist attractions, and they all made sure to get their kicks while listening to Bobby Troup's popular anthem. Route 66 prospered through the 1950s as America's passionate love affair with the internal combustion engine intensified.

In the mid-1950s, with big, gas-guzzling cars popular, President Dwight D. Eisenhower decided the nation needed more superhighways to handle the increase in traffic. Although this signaled the decline of the fabled path known as "America's Main Street," Route 66 enjoyed many more years of celebrity. The building of the new federal highways, including the interstates destined to replace Route 66, was slow and laborious. The last stretch of Route 66 was finally bypassed in 1984.

Yet even as familiar shield signs were removed and road maps changed, there remained people who knew Route 66 would never die. These protectors of pop culture, commercial archaeologists, preservationists, and historians joined ranks with the dedicated folks who still eked out a living along the highway. Together they kept the lights burning and traffic moving through the highway's years of decline. About 1990, a revival of passionate interest in Route 66 began to blossom. That revival not only continues today but has gathered momentum.

Along much of the more than 85 percent of Route 66 that remains today, nothing has changed. In other places, where change has occurred, badly needed improvements have often been made. Travelers can still find the genuine article. They can still find examples of all the road's incarnations—including motels, curio shops, greasy spoons, and pie palaces—where generous helpings of hospitality have been served for generations.

Authentic oases, many of them family-owned, still turn out real food. These are meals cooked on the premises, not bland turnpike fare or franchise food served in Styrofoam boxes. Diners eager to rid themselves of hunger pangs can sit at a counter and watch their meal prepared before their eyes. Biscuits are served piping hot and there are lumps in the mashed potatoes. Nothing is instant but the service. As the Puritan poet Edward Taylor might have put it, had he sat down to a blue plate special, "It is food too fine for angels."

Nothing is predictable on Route 66. There is plenty of adventure. The potential for an escapade lurks around every curve and bend in the road, which accounts for much of the old road's attraction. For a multitude of travelers, from across the nation as well as a growing number from Europe and the Pacific Rim, this is an American highway that will never die.

Route 66 has evolved into a revered icon. It is a destination in and of itself. A trek down the highway is mandatory for all those who find time sacred and want to experience the America that used to be — America before the nation became generic.

The road of John Steinbeck, Will Rogers, Dorothea Lange, Woody Guthrie, and Jack Kerouac is still the best path for dreamers, drifters, and ramblers on a quest. The revival grows larger and gains momentum. The Mother Road is stronger than ever. The old road has new meaning and life.

Route 66 is a neon journey down a passageway of memory. It is a road that helped shape America's history and culture. Driving the highway today not only promises adventure but also evokes feelings of fantasy and romance. It gives the traveler a sense of personal involvement.

There have been many books published about Route 66, and many photographers, including a few of the best, have presented their own interpretations of the Mother Road. This particular book, produced by photographers Jane Bernard and Polly Brown, is unlike any other. Each photograph here stands alone yet is important to the others. There is not a single cull in the lot. Some of the images are gritty. Others are as smooth as a cup of fresh custard. All of them capture the attitudes and values of the subjects. A single look into the faces and eyes reveals much.

The combination of the straightforward images accompanied by the actual voices of the people portrayed delivers a potent one-two punch. These are honest photographs and words. They do not lie. Together they expose a true slice of America — a nation of movement and energy.

This book shows us people living in secret corners and hidden towns that can still be found if travelers merely dare to exit the interstate highway. To do that, they have to believe that life begins at the off-ramp. Then, with the windows rolled down and the radio playing, they can open their eyes to the past and, just maybe, discover something of themselves.

It is a journey worth taking.

Enjoy the ride.

—MICHAEL WALLIS
Author of *Route 66: The Mother Road*

A BOW OF GRATITUDE to our Route 66 mentor, author Michael Wallis, who believed in this project from its beginnings, generously helped us through its many turns, always validated our work, and gave us the honor of writing the foreword to our book. We are also grateful to one of our first cheerleaders, Rich Williams, former president of the New Mexico Route 66 Association, who backed up his kind words with real help and support; and to Wade Patterson at the New Mexico Endowment for the Humanities, who patiently led us step by step through the daunting task of writing a grant proposal. Mary Virginia Swanson's extensive expertise was invaluable in helping us get this project supported and published.

Many people in the Route 66 community help contribute to this project's success. David and Mary Lou Knudson of the National Historic Route 66 Federation provided us with contacts and encouragement to cover the whole road, instead of just the western states, as we had first planned. Route 66 author and chairman of the Preservation Committee of the Route 66 Association of Illinois, John Weiss, shared his extensive knowledge of Illinois with us. During our many miles of road travel the following people provided us with gracious hospitality: Ginger Gallager from the Red Cedar Inn and John Marbury from the Ranch Kitchen fed us delicious and memorable meals; Evan Bernard helped us to navigate in and around Santa Monica and Los Angeles and treated us to dinner; Ramona Lehman and Susan and Garrett Schniewind provided us with a place to stay; and Connie and Mike Irby rolled out their red carpet to give us a home away from home while we were in Oklahoma.

Thanks are also due to those who helped us with the many details that go into a project of this magnitude. Without them we would still be slogging through the material. Marlys Fick has our undying gratitude for her dedication and hard work on this project; her contributions are too numerous to mention here. Myrna Bernard, Jane's mother, as is her style, went above and beyond the call of parental duty to transcribe many of our interviews. David Jondreau patiently and cheerfully helped us with computer glitches; without him we would have torn all of our hair out. Alex Chamberlin and Corrine Padilla helped us frame

Acknowledgments

and mat seventy-three of our images for exhibition. LeAnne Summers helped us organize promotional material. Joseph Campos, Ralph Richards, and Marie Mazon graciously participated in our panel discussion on Route 66 and the importance of community.

We are grateful to those who had faith in us early on in this process and generously supported us by purchasing prints of our images before the work was completed: Sam and Nancy Billard, Barry and Myrna Bernard, Sam and Bertha Britt, Mike Glass, Lynn Laier and Steve Benjamin, Deb and Ken LeClair, Geoffrey Kimball, Steve Lipsey, Mark Mason, Lois Meisler, Carol Norton, Connie and Jim Pollak, Robert and Elise Pratt, John Sandoval, George and Francis Schultz, Joe Schwerin, Philip Sharples, Rick and Sandra Webel, Doug Windsor, and Walter Wright. Additional support came from Carol and Norton Fishman, Charlotte Ward, Artie Pratt, Claire Warhaftig, and Pauline Webel. Deborah Light of the Thanks Be to Grandmother Winifred Foundation supported Polly. Thank you all. This project took wings because of your generosity.

For their unwavering encouragement and support over the last several years, we are grateful to David Fowler, Polly's husband, and to Jane's boyfriend, Peter Prince. They were gracious about the invasion of Route 66 on their lives (and in David's case, home turf) and our numerous absences.

We would like to thank the following authors whose writings have been invaluable resources throughout this project: Michael Wallis (*Route 66: The Mother Road*), Tom Snyder (*Route 66 Traveler's Guide and Roadside Companion*), Tom Teague (*Searching for 66*), John Weiss (*Traveling the New, Historic Route 66 of Illinois*), and Thomas Arthur Repp (*Route 66: The Empires of Amusement*).

To the talented staff at the Museum of New Mexico Press we extend many thanks. Mary Wachs, our editor, was enthusiastic about this project from the start. Her professionalisim, good humor, unique insight, and wisdom helped craft the final product. Press Director Anna Gallegos patiently sat through several contract meetings will us and stood calmly by while we hyperventilated over the details. Our talented designer David Skolkin took our mountain of material and organized it into dynamic form.

ROAD JOURNEYS HAVE LONG OCCUPIED a central place in the American psyche, and America's first highway symbolizes the ultimate road trip. The myth of the Mother Road is one of romance, adventure, and apple pie but the reality is more complex.

When we began researching this book, we knew next to nothing about Route 66. However, we shared a passion for making photographs and an interest in people's stories. We were motivated by the possibilities of the open road and hoped to experience America without preconceptions or prejudice.

At the start of the project, Jane had recently returned from an extended stay in Eastern Europe. She found herself grateful to be an American and full of renewed interest in her country. Polly had moved from New England to the Southwest and was questioning the connection between identity and place. For three years the two of us traveled along the road. Route 66 provided us with an opportunity to explore the cultural and visual landscape of our nation. It gave us a point of departure and an invitation to embark on our own personal journey, a journey that would connect us to America.

For three years we traveled along the road. Our purpose in undertaking this project was to document how the heritage of Route 66 is reflected in current conditions and rhythms of life and to portray the road with a fresh spin on local folklore and Americana. We wanted to find out what it is to travel Route 66 today and to visually respond to whatever and whomever we might find along the way.

There is great visual variety in the landscape. The green trees and fields of Illinois and Missouri gradually give way to the rolling plains of Oklahoma and Texas, which in turn become the stark and beautiful deserts of New Mexico and Arizona. Missouri is lush. Illinois has tidy and well-manicured little towns. St. Louis has beautiful stone houses. California has palm trees and the ocean. In short, each state has its own special qualities and surprises.

Introduction

Driving Route 66 made us realize how dramatically road travel has changed in a relatively short period of time. Early travelers making their way west found driving to be a major undertaking, often full of uncertainty. Road conditions were rough and the journey was taxing to early automobiles.

Even today, in air-conditioned vehicles, a trip through the Mojave Desert is an adventure. During most of the year, if you stop and step out into the landscape, you can, quite literally, fry. Standing on a hot, remote roadside one April gave us a whole new perspective on just how fearsome the experience must have been for early travelers. The passes through the desert are formidable, the landscape barren almost beyond imagining, and the weather extremely unforgiving.

It's hard to imagine a time when our current highway system did not exist, but before the construction of Route 66 there were few connecting roads. Communities were effectively much further apart. The advent of Route 66 played a major role in changing the demographics of this nation. Not only did the new highway make it possible for people to connect with those in nearby communities, it also facilitated migration to distant parts of this huge land. The development of the road was a boon to the economy, making it easier for farmers to haul their crops to market. The distribution of goods became more efficient and produce easily available and more affordable.

In 1925 a government board was formed to design a highway system loosely based on a grid template Thomas Jefferson had envisioned more than a century before. By the mid-twenties the automobile had begun to change habits of daily life in America, creating a demand for new and improved roadways. Route 66 was commissioned in 1926 to connect Chicago to Los Angeles, making it the first highway to reach the west coast.

Today the old highway is a patchwork of pavement that weaves through new development and interstate highways. In some places it no longer exists. Locating the true Mother

Road always involves a fair amount of head scratching, consulting of maps, talking to locals, and navigating by intuition. One comes to notice the telltale signs: the curve of the road, Route 66–era buildings, icons, and signage.

Route 66 extended 2,400 miles through three time zones and eight states. It was a road of flight, commerce, and inspiration. During the depression years, it became a passage west, a lifeline for families desperate to reach California and a chance of survival.

Our identities as photographers have been strongly influenced by the poignant images of Farm Security Administration photographers such as Walker Evans, Dorothea Lange, and Russell Lee. Even so, as we encountered people who had actually witnessed those families moving west along Route 66, we found the Dust Bowl era ceased to be a distant abstraction and became instead a living history lesson.

It is difficult for Americans to envision the widespread migration of a whole people. True, we are accustomed to television images of refugee populations in foreign lands. But imagine waves of men, women, and children passing through your own town in search of a better life. Our travels made us vividly aware of the great migration that took place in this country in the 1930s and the fact that the United States had its own internal refugee population less than a century ago.

Poverty continues to be part of our society but not nearly as dramatically or visibly as during the depression years. People whom we met who had been in business along Route 66 for many years recounted stories of people who had knocked on their doors well after the Dust Bowl era was over and asked for milk. One woman told us she was relieved to discover, after the highway had been decommissioned, that desperate people no longer sought her out.

During World War II, Route 66 was used to move troops east and west. After the war was over, Bobby Troup wrote his famous song "Get Your Kicks on Route 66." It was recorded by almost everyone, it seemed, and glorified the heyday of the Mother Road in the 1950s and 1960s. Those were years when Americans had more security and were on the move. People increasingly traveled for pleasure, obeying Detroit's command to "See the USA in your Chevrolet!" Route 66 came to represent freedom, adventure, and, for some, one more chance. The Mother Road put Americans in touch with America. It was the source of the myth of the open road.

Eight decades of travelers passing through small towns and rural communities provided a boon to local businesses and commerce. A road culture was created. When the interstate system replaced Route 66, those towns along the highway felt the impact both physically and economically. "It was as if a brick wall had been put up," said Jerry Hughes, a waitress who has lived and worked on Route 66 all her life. Since the road was decommissioned, these towns have struggled to redefine their identities and economies.

Most travel today has become impersonal: We head from Point A to Point B as quickly as possible, stopping to eat and refuel at "Anywhere, USA" franchise chains. Every town seems to have an identical strip of Denny's and Burger Kings. No matter where we are, it looks the same. We hear every day how big businesses are swallowing smaller ones in corporate America. But nearly three-quarters of all firms in the United States still have no payroll, and businesses with fewer than twenty employees provide over twenty million Americans with a paycheck.

In the past decade there has been a rebirth of interest in and travel on the Mother Road. All along Route 66, cafes and service stations, motels and diners are experiencing a surge in business as travelers rediscover the old highway. In doing so, they breathe new life into roadside communities.

Traveling Route 66 offers a respite from predictable, homogenized, mainstream American life and a welcome antidote to the ubiquitous sprawl of our land. It was tremendously refreshing to us to patronize businesses that were not part of a chain or owned by a conglomerate. We realized how important such enterprises still are in the socioeconomic makeup of this country. Over and over, we talked to people who had gone their own way. They had chosen to run their own small business instead of working at a huge discount store, or they served their own cooking instead of becoming a manager at a fast-food chain.

The identity of Route 66 was built on such locally owned and run establishments, and that remains true to this day. Many of our favorite memories of our travels are our visits with the proprietors of local cafes. These men and women truly care about their customers and usually have interesting stories to tell and valuable information to share about the road.

On one of our first trips on Route 66, we used a ten-year-old book as our guide. To our dismay, we found that the Club Café in Santa Rosa, New Mexico, which we had read about, no longer existed. However, as we explored the town we discovered that the "Fatman" logo, a trademark of the Club Café, had been adopted by Joseph's Restaurant just down the road.

While Route 66 purists may find such changes disconcerting, the reality of life is that our world is constantly evolving. So, too, is Route 66. While many classic and well-loved icons such as Manny Goodman's Covered Wagon Trading Post in Albuquerque, New Mexico, and Lucille's Gas Station in Hydro, Oklahoma, no longer exist, other vital businesses (and business owners) have emerged to take their place and carry on the Route 66 traditions of friendliness and hospitality in new ways. Some, like Suresh Patel, owner of the Wigwam Motel in Rialto, California, are resurrecting and restoring well-loved icons of old. Others, such as Robert Erwin, owner of Goff's General Store in the Mojave Desert in Essex, California, have built new businesses that provide services for travelers in the true spirit of the Mother Road.

Some of our favorite encounters, such as having lunch with trucker Richard Bruce in California, we could not possibly have planned for. Bruce drives sections of old Route 66 while making deliveries for Save the Children. Another special pleasure was meeting Ruby Boswell, who is close to one hundred years old, in Pontiac, Illinois. Boswell witnessed the building of the original Route 66 with horses and mules and today has a business repairing and caning furniture.

Our many adventures on Route 66 uncovered diverse communities that portray a microcosm of America today. As always, when one scratches any superficial veneer, one reveals gaps between myth and reality. There are potholes in the road to the American dream. The old demons of poverty, racism, and alienation are with us still.

Several people we met talked about having experienced racism in their communities and described how local attitudes have evolved over the years. One older man recalled that a public pool had been built nearby with an accompanying sign that read "For the Children of the Local County" but that his children had been barred from swimming there because of their race. He had always felt that was unfair and was happy to see the day when his grandchildren were allowed to swim in that same pool.

For the most part, we found hardworking folks along Route 66, people trying as best they could to make do. To us, these men and women symbolize American ingenuity and determination. They were generous, helpful, and had a genuine desire to share their stories. These people are the lifeblood of Route 66. They represent a link not only to the past but also to the heart of twenty-first-century America.

JANE BERNARD (LEFT) AND POLLY BROWN
AT SAND HILLS CURIOSITY SHOP,
ERICK, OKLAHOMA.

Riviera Restaurant

WE DRIVE THROUGH THE LUSH SPRING COUNTRYSIDE of northern Illinois, where small towns and rural fields convey a sense of order. There are exact rows of newly planted crops, the lawns are mowed short, and the cars parked in the driveways appear perfectly aligned.

Earlier in the day we met with John Weiss, author of *The Historic Route 66 of Illinois Guidebook*. At the end of our meeting he said, "Be sure to eat at the Riviera Restaurant tonight and say hello to Bob and Peggy. You must order 'Shrimp de Jonge,' Peggy's specialty. No trip on Route 66 is complete without the Riviera experience."

That is where we're headed now. The Riviera is an original Route 66 roadhouse. It's been in operation since the 1930s, when movie stars and mobsters came here to eat and drink. Bob and Peggy Kraft have been its proprietors since 1972.

We pull into the parking lot and look for an entrance to the white frame house. As we circle the building, we notice an old, unrestored streetcar in the backyard. Still no entrance.

Finally we descend some stairs into what looks like a basement and enter a cave-like room. There is a long bar on one side and maybe a dozen tables covered with plastic tablecloths. At one of those tables sits a group of older men. They look as if they have been there all day. The ceiling is low, with white stalactite-like protrusions pointing down into the room, and the pipes are visible overhead. The room reminds us of a 1950s rec room.

We take a seat at the bar, where Bob is busy vigorously shaking a cocktail. He insists on giving us a drink as he starts telling us about his and Peggy's years at the Riviera. Behind him, on the back wall of the bar, hang six or more framed maxims along the lines of "Save Water — Drink Booze" and "Lead Me not into Temptation, for I Shall Find it Myself." On the counter behind the bar are huge stacks of papers and receipts, apparently documenting the Riviera's entire life span.

Illinois

In the meantime, Peggy moves from table to table taking orders and serving food. She then returns to the bar in an effort to keep Bob's Riviera stories honest.

Bob tells us that during the depression years, a hobo who was passing through looking for work was hired by the owners to create the plaster stalactites over the bar. "We have female names for all of them," says Bob. We note that they do resemble mammary glands more than they do stalactites.

To Peggy's delight, we order her Shrimp de Jonge. "I created this recipe myself," she says proudly, "and everyone seems to love it." When dinner is ready it is sent down from the upstairs kitchen on a dumbwaiter operated by a rope.

The Shrimp de Jonge is not for the faint of heart or for those concerned about their cholesterol count. As we are neither we happily devour our servings.

When we finally leave the cave room to return to our motel, our stomachs are full and our heads are swimming with stories. We feel as if we have just been in a 1950s time warp and paid a visit to the *Twilight Zone*.

BOB AND PEGGY KRAFT,
RIVIERA RESTAURANT, GARDNER, ILLINOIS
POLLY BROWN

BOB:

I was born in 1924. Peggy and I have had the Riviera Restaurant since 1972, and I've been tending bar for fifty-three years, twenty-five in Chicago and twenty-eight out here. Peggy and I get along great, but she works too hard. She's the worker, and I'm the drinker. She does a good job of working, and I do a good job of drinking. I know that she has to love me or she couldn't stand me.

PEGGY:
That's for sure.

THE WILLOWBROOK BALLROOM,
WILLOW SPRINGS, ILLINOIS
POLLY BROWN

The Willowbrook Ballroom has been a Midwest entertainment landmark since 1921. It was founded by John Verderbar as an outdoor dance hall known as "Oh Henry Park." In exchange for naming the establishment after its new "Oh Henry" candy bar, the Williamson Candy Company of Chicago agreed to help cover start-up costs and provide a yearly subsidy payment.

The dance hall flourished through the 1920s until disaster struck and the complex burned to the ground. Out of the ashes rose the "Oh Henry Ballroom." In the 1930s and 1940s, people were in the mood to swing, and the ballroom became home to some of the biggest bands of the day, complete with its own restaurant, soda fountain, and flower shop.

By the 1950s, a series of additional lounges and restaurants had been added. Eventually, the entire complex simply became known as "The Willowbrook."

Today, depending on the night, dancers can West Coast swing, ballroom dance, country line dance, or salsa.

24

had a gas station and raised four kids here. In 1985 we had to get rid of the gas tanks, so I took a job as a security supervisor at the nuclear power plant. I worked there for eight years and thought I was set, but then they had a reduction in the work force. I was fifty-nine-and-a-half, and they put me out on the streets. I mowed lawns all that summer.

When I was doing bodywork, I kept spare car and truck bumpers, and I used to make little things. Between mowing jobs, I started cutting up bumpers and making animals. Then I started collecting farm parts. When I got a job at a machine shop, I started bringing home shavings. From shavings, I got the idea for the spray foam insulation. Now when I make my animal sculptures I mix my mediums together.

The first piece I made was that grasshopper over there. I asked my neighbor to help me carry it out. He said it would have to be after dark because he was afraid that someone would see him. He thought they would think he was nuts like me.

People started to stop and admire the pieces. Some would say, "Boy, isn't that beautiful!" so I just kept on making them. There are a lot of tourists coming off Route 66, but I'm not here every day. I have a phone number, so if someone is really serious they call me and I meet them here. But my neighbors tell me there are people here all the time.

I get very attached to my pieces. They are kind of like my kids, and I can't sell my kids. If a customer comes along and he talks to me right and doesn't make fun of the art, and if I say a piece is X dollars and he doesn't say something stupid, I might sell it to him, or her if I'm dealing with a woman. I have to feel my art is going to a good home.

In 1994 these people came in driving a big ol' Cadillac. The woman asked me, "Are you the artist"? It was the first time I had heard myself called that. "Art"? I thought, "Art" was that fella I grew up with.

JACK BARKER,
METAL ARTIST, ESSEX, ILLINOIS
POLLY BROWN

This has been a family-owned business since 1923, three years before Route 66 was commissioned. It was just a small, one-man-show dinner routine. The original owner was Greek and he went by William Mitchell, but his real name was Michapoulos.

My mom Kathryn and my brother Nick and I bought the business from Uncle Lou in the early 1990s. My mom does the administrative stuff and works in the restaurant on Sundays because that's my day off. My brother manages Lou Mitchell's Express at the airport, plus he comes and hangs out with me because it's fun.

People get off the train or the bus and are told, "If you are tired or hungry, you've got to go to Lou Mitchell's." Some people have read about us in a book, and some have been coming here since they were born. Now they're sixty-five and they bring their grandkids. For them, coming here is like coming home to their grandmother's house.

Our restaurant is like how it was in the old days. This is where people come when they want to feel safe and happy and comforted and share how they are feeling. I tell everyone who comes in here, "Good morning, welcome to Lou Mitchell's," and I really want to know how they are. That's old-time stuff and I kind of like that. Besides, this is my party.

HELEEN THANAS,
GENERAL MANAGER, LOU MITCHELL'S RESTAURANT
AND BAKERY, CHICAGO, ILLINOIS

POLLY BROWN

RICH HENRY,
HENRY'S OLD ROUTE 66
RABBIT RANCH, STAUNTON, ILLINOIS
JANE BERNARD

My dad was a truck driver, and some of my fondest memories are driving old Route 66 with my dad in his rig. He ran a lot between St. Louis and Chicago. I loved visiting the different truck stops with him. I remember the knick-knack souvenirs that they sold and visiting with the different drivers that we'd meet along the way. The old truck stops were nothing like the ones you see today. They were just little bitty buildings with a café on one side and maybe a counter and a few tables. That's what we kind of fashioned our building here after.

Some of the things I have in the museum are toys from my childhood. We have a little bit of everything and a lot of gas station memorabilia. My wife and I have a real love of the Mother Road. We like for people to be able to have a sense of Route 66, especially the younger generation. If we don't educate them, they'll never know what it was all about.

We have miniature bunnies that give entertainment to travelers. We'd rather have those than buffalos and rattlesnakes. We also have a number of Volkswagen Rabbits, and some day we plan on planting about eight of them in the ground, kind of like Cadillac Ranch.

We farm a pretty good-sized lot, about 1,900 acres, but farming is very difficult now. Prices for the crops we grow — wheat, soybeans, and corn — have been low, well below profitable levels. We're still recovering from low hog prices a few years ago. They got down to ten cents a pound, and it takes thirty to forty cents to break even. Many farmers went out of business, and if it weren't for government support we'd all be out of business.

The fact is that we produce more than people need. Sadly, there are countries around the world where people are starving, but they don't have enough money to buy our food.

We sell our grain to local elevators or grain terminals in this part of the country, and they sell it to others. A large amount of Illinois grain stays in state, but a fair amount also gets exported. The soybeans are used as a protein in human food, and the oil is used for making plastics.

We farmers are really trying to push the use of ethanol as an energy source in place of gasoline. We can take the food products out of corn and still use the rest of it for ethanol. Gasohol is only 10 percent ethanol and 90 percent gasoline. But you can actually burn 85 percent ethanol and not be so dependent on gasoline.

LEE MARTEN,
FARMER AND SON OF FRANCIS MARTEN,
ORIGINAL CARETAKER OF OUR LADY OF
THE HIGHWAY SHRINE, RAYMOND, ILLINOIS
JANE BERNARD

POLK-A-DOT DRIVE INN,
BRAIDWOOD, ILLINOIS

JANE BERNARD

The original Polk-a-Dot opened in 1956 when a man named Chet parked a white bus painted with polka dots on the lot and served fast food through two of its windows. Judy Chinski and her sister-in-law, Cathy Dixon, bought the place in 1987 and renovated the drive-in.

HISTORIC STANDARD OIL FILLING STATION, ODELL, ILLINOIS

JANE BERNARD

I was born in 1904. Still driving. Here's my license. Got my little Chevy out there in the driveway.

Before they built old Route 66, we had a little section of about two or three miles of paved road just outside of town. It was just a little narrow strip and, oh my gosh, people were beginning to get cars at that time. They'd come by riding on that new hard road; it was a big deal. When they started talking about building this road straight through, why, we thought that was really exciting. But, of course, we were poor. For years we never thought we would ever own a car.

Route 66 was quite a sensation. It was one lane to begin with, but people thought they were lucky to get that. You had to squeeze, but cars could pass. Used to be that if you got a rainy spell and the roads were getting muddy, you couldn't drive. So an all-weather road made a big change in traveling.

I went to school here. I had good teachers and wonderful classmates. I got along well and never had many problems. I did have a few bad times on account of prejudice. We were segregated at the movies. In the theater, all the black people had to sit in the balcony. There were a lot of restaurants where we couldn't go. I couldn't get my hair cut at the barbershop here; I had to go out of town. But the school was integrated. I always said that there weren't enough black people here in Pontiac to warrant a separate school, or I think they would have had one. But that was my experience.

But, thank God, things have changed. I can't hold a grudge because in my lifetime people have been so nice and helpful. Even helped me get this home. Hell, I've had help all along, so I've got a lot to be thankful for. So far, I've enjoyed life and had a wonderful family. Everything has been good to me. You have to admit that those unfair things happened, but all in all it's been pleasant. I praise the Lord for letting me be around, because it could have been a lot worse.

RUBY BOSWELL,
RUBY'S CHAIR CANING, PONTIAC, ILLINOIS

JANE BERNARD

MRS. WILLARD MARBURGER,

MOUNT OLIVE, ILLINOIS

POLLY BROWN

Meramec Caverns in Stanton, Missouri, were commercially developed in the 1930s by Lester Dill. A creative self-promoter, Dill posted signs on barns in as many as forty states. He and his crew scoured the countryside to locate just the right barns with just the right visibility. He enticed farmers into the deal by offering to paint their barns for free and handing out watches, whiskey, chocolates, and free passes to the caverns.

    There are two remaining Meramec Caverns barns along Route 66 in Illinois, and both have been restored by volunteers from the Route 66 Association of Illinois Historic Preservation Committee.

MERAMEC CAVERNS BARN, OLD ROUTE 66
AND INTERSTATE 55, ILLINOIS

JANE BERNARD

GLAIDA, STEVE, MIKE, AND DEBBIE FUNK,

FUNK'S GROVE MAPLE SIRUP, SHIRLEY, ILLINOIS

POLLY BROWN

GLAIDA FUNK:

In 1824 my husband Steve's great-grandfather settled here, and they made sirup for their own use as a sweetener. Spelling sirup with an "i" became our trademark. Everyone thinks we've misspelled it, but Webster's says the preferred spelling was "i," and the U.S. Dept. of Agriculture used "i."

We starting making our sirup in 1948. We hung about five hundred taps that first year, and then we started increasing until now we hang about 6,500. Those first years the sap house was pretty primitive. It had dirt floors, and we cooked with wood. We had electricity but we didn't have water, so when the sap house roof caught fire we had to use sap to put it out. At that time we sold the sirup right from our back porch.

I remember before the interstate bypassed us that we had so many people stopping off Route 66. Not only customers but also hitchhikers and vagrants. We always let the vagrants work for food. Many people stopped because their car broke down or they were out of gas. This one couple came in the other day and said that when they were dating they were out on Route 66 one Christmas Eve and got a flat. We came out and changed it for them, and they have never forgotten that.

When the interstate was built in 1976 our business declined and we had a rough couple of years, but eventually people found us and business picked up. This has always been a real family affair, and we've been fortunate in having all our kids and their spouses live within twenty miles of here, so we can drag them out anytime we need help. Now we do a mail-order business all over the world.

'm a back-roads traveler, always have been. I drive convertibles and stay away from the expressways. Route 66 is all back roads.

The purpose of preservation is to save symbols of time and place. If we don't preserve the little icons and pieces of the road then there's nothing to enjoy. How many kids know what a gravity-flow gas pump is? Convenience stores and Twinkies, that's what they understand. They don't know Mom and Pop and apple pie. We have traded all of that for Ronald McDonald, you might say.

What better symbol is there of Route 66 than an old filling station? This 1932 Standard Oil filling station in Odell, Illinois, has so much character to it. We decided that it would make a good project for our preservation committee. Everyone said it was too far gone and called us fools, but we went ahead and did it anyhow.

There were big holes in the roof and the place was falling down. A small group of us pooled our money and bought some plastic and climbed up on the roof. We almost killed ourselves. We patched the roof and the wind blew it off, so we went up and patched it again. That bought us the time that we needed to get the community involved. The town took out a loan to purchase the property. We've had fundraisers, sold pieces of pie, had poker runs, taken donations of any kind, sold T-shirts: whatever it takes.

Little by little, we have gotten many people involved. It isn't unusual now for thirty to fifty people to show up for a work session. Everybody wants to be part of our preservation projects, since we've proven we can do it.

The Odell Station was recognized in 2001 as the best preservation project on all of Route 66. We're proud of that fact. From something that everyone said couldn't be done to being the best on the road: That's quite an accomplishment.

I know it sounds as if we're bragging about what we've done, but the story is really about the people who came out here and helped make a project like this happen. They wanted to be part of saving a piece of history. Isn't that neat?

JOHN WEISS,
CHAIRMAN OF THE PRESERVATION COMMITTEE
OF THE ROUTE 66 ASSOCIATION OF ILLINOIS,
STANDARD OIL FILLING STATION, ODELL, ILLINOIS

POLLY BROWN

Precious Moments Chapel

Before traveling Route 66 in Missouri, we were unaware of the existence of Precious Moments Chapel and theme park in Carthage. That quickly changes once we cross the state line. Whenever the chapel comes up in conversation, it invariably invokes the same response. The person speaking pauses, cocks his or her head at a slight angle, and says in hushed tones, "Isn't it beautiful?"

The Precious Moments Chapel was created by Precious Moments artist Sam Butcher. For the uninitiated, Precious Moments products feature big-eyed children. Their images grace greeting cards, are available as porcelain bisque statues, and can be purchased at Hallmark stores everywhere. The figures are allegedly the most popular collectibles in the United States.

We are skeptical about spending time at Precious Moments, but our good friend Michael Wallis, who has never steered us wrong, insists we stop there. On a rainy afternoon we drive up to the Precious Moments complex. We weave our way through a maze of signs directing visitors to the Precious Moments Wedding Island, Convention Center, Theater, Museum, and Welcome Center. The place is overwhelming.

Mechanized Precious Moments figures wave to us from every corner of the welcome center, prompting a brief *déjà vu* of the "It's a Small World" ride at Disneyland. The welcome center also includes a buffet and a series of gift shops. Of course, the gift shop sells every possible product featuring big-eyed children.

A covered tram takes visitors from the welcome center to the attractions. The driver seems stunned when we thank him for the offer of a ride but say we'd rather walk. Maybe walkers are a rare breed at Precious Moments. We pass through beautifully manicured gardens and the "Avenue of Angels," which is graced with statues of big-eyed cherubim and seraphim.

The main doors of the chapel are covered with carvings of Bible scenes populated with big-eyed children. As ornate as they are, they leave us unprepared for what lies beyond.

Frescos several stories high cover the walls and ceiling. The scenes are from the Old and New Testaments, and the characters are all big-eyed children and big-eyed angels. A series of paintings portrays the seven days of the Creation, and "Let There Be Light" features

Missouri

two round-cheeked, big-eyed angels holding flashlights. Our mouths hang open, and we are speechless. The magnitude of it all is stunning.

We later learn that artist Sam Butcher was inspired by a visit to the Sistine Chapel. One can only imagine the look on Michelangelo's face if he had been able to witness the glory of Precious Moments Chapel.

PRECIOUS MOMENTS CHAPEL,
CARTHAGE, MISSOURI

JANE BERNARD

GLEN E. WRINKLE,
WRINK'S MARKET, LEBANON, MISSOURI

JANE BERNARD

They used to say that Route 66 was the Main Street of America. It's more so now than it ever was, and for the whole world. We didn't use to get all these foreigners traveling Route 66. They come in, and we just have a ball. They can't always understand me, and I don't always understand them, but we've got this sign language. And, you know, if they aren't happy, we make them happy, so they leave smiling. They can't get away from it.

JAMMING AT MOLLY'S,

ST. LOUIS, MISSOURI

POLLY BROWN

EXOTIC ANIMAL PARADISE,

STRAFFORD, MISSOURI

POLLY BROWN

always looked like Elvis, even when I was a teenager. I was born not too far from where he lived in Tennessee.

I've worked construction most of my life, but I've always been a country singer. When my hair turned gray about ten years ago, I didn't think anything of it. Then four years ago I dyed it black, and everyone was amazed at how much I looked like Elvis. So I started doing Elvis gigs, and everyone loved me. I was so successful that I started looking for a place that I could do Elvis shows all the time. In 2001 I opened this restaurant, and my Elvis shows here have been very popular.

TERRY MAPLES,
ELVIS IMPERSONATOR,
CUBA, MISSOURI
POLLY BROWN

KATHERINE:

I came to work at the Red Cedar when I was nineteen, and I met my husband James Smith here. His uncle and his dad built this place. If my husband were still alive, we'd be married sixty years now.

We rented the place out for a while, but now our daughter Ginger runs it. She's done a good job. She likes this kind of stuff, and she works herself to death. If you went into her kitchen, you wouldn't be afraid to eat anything here. Ginger and her partner, Wes, are doing a beautiful job. I come down here and watch them work, and they've got everything under control.

The logs in this building came from my father-in-law's farm. We have a lot of people coming in here saying they can smell cedar. That's imagination because you can't smell cedar anymore. These are old logs, and they haven't been rechinked since it's been built. Can you imagine?

GINGER:

I've been running the restaurant since October 1987. Back then, people came in wanting the same foods that Mom and Dad served. When I asked Mom how she made the dumplings for the chicken and dumplings, her answer was, "You've seen me make these for thirty years. You should know how to do this." I've learned that she just doesn't remember.

We sell a lot of prime rib and we get a lot of compliments on our steaks. Filet mignon is my favorite. My partner, Wes, knows how to cook the steaks and season them. We sell a lot of fried chicken. We buy fresh, keep our oil fresh, and make many things from scratch.

When I first started working here, I was in high school, about fifteen or sixteen years old. I remember the day the bypass opened in 1961. It was like "The Twilight Zone": One day you were busy and the next day there was hardly anybody around. But within a year business was back, better than ever, because this part of Route 66 is a service road.

When I was a child, we lived on the other side of the dining room wall. It seemed like every night as I went to sleep, someone played "Midnight Serenade" by Glenn Miller on the jukebox. It was almost as if that song was playing just for me. When I hear it now, as an adult, it's soothing, and it brings back good memories.

GINGER GALLAGER AND KATHERINE SMITH,
RED CEDAR INN, PACIFIC, MISSOURI
POLLY BROWN

My husband Bob and I came from northeast Iowa in 1971. We'd been farmers, and we had had a terrible winter. We went to Springfield, Missouri, and looked at four motels. On the way back, we stopped in Lebanon, and the next thing we know we're over here at the Munger Moss. We spent an hour and a half talking to the owners, Pete and Jessy Hudson. A couple of days later, we made an offer.

We left Iowa on May 30. My oldest daughter was just starting junior high school, my baby was seven, and I was young too. We sat there and cried, me and my four kids. We were leaving everything that we had known and going to what seemed like a strange country.

Pete and Jessy were like another mom and dad to us. They taught us the ropes. Pete came down with cancer and died a few years later, but to this day he is still here with me. When times get hard, he's sitting on my shoulder saying, "Hey, kid, you'll make it. This place has always made it. It will continue to make it. Believe me. I've gone through it all."

My kids took to motel living and learned to fend for themselves. My baby had been scared of water up in Iowa, but after two weeks here he was diving off the deep end of the pool. One afternoon the maids came to me about a room that had a "Do Not Disturb" sign on it. What should they do? When they finally went in, they found my two boys watching television.

The kids all pitched in. At that time, there were seventy-two rooms renting for $9 each. Both the boys and girls learned to take out the trash and carry things for the maids. They were also goodwill ambassadors and attached themselves to anyone who came through the door.

It wasn't until 1987 that I became aware of the importance of Route 66 to the motel and our business. That's when I met my first "roadologist," and he started telling me about Michael Wallis and Tom Snyder and their work on the Mother Road. We started having guests looking for old Route 66.

I love Route 66 people. I've never met one of them who was snooty or mean. They are down to earth, and they love history. It doesn't matter if they are from Europe, Japan, Australia or the United States. They are all just good people.

RAMONA LEHMAN,

MUNGER MOSS MOTEL,

LEBANON, MISSOURI

POLLY BROWN

BOOTS MOTEL, CARTHAGE, MISSOURI

JANE BERNARD

The Boots Motel was built by Arthur Boots in 1939. Clark Gable,
Gene Autry, and Smiley Burnett all slept here.

66 DRIVE-IN THEATER, CARTHAGE, MISSOURI

JANE BERNARD

ROUTE 66 LOUNGE,
CUBA, MISSOURI

JANETTE AND ROXANNE SASS,

GRANNY'S BIRD HOUSE, ROLLA, MISSOURI

POLLY BROWN

THE CYCLONES, AAA MISSOURI STATE CHAMPIONS,
CROSS ROADS CAFÉ, DONIPHAN, MISSOURI

JANE BERNARD

We opened our first roller rink in a building downtown on Commercial Street in 1942. That was when I began to skate. I did artistic skating and entered competitions and won pins and medals. I went on to become a contest judge and hosted a lot of benefits for charity. The skaters put on exhibitions, and the receipts were donated to a particular charity. Every February, I held a "Queen of Hearts" contest. Usually about twenty girls skated, and they were judged on their skating ability, beauty, and gracefulness. It was quite an honor for the girl who was crowned queen.

The first half of the week, we rent to organizations like churches and schools for their private parties. We've had as many as three parties in twenty-four hours. The public skating is toward the end of the week. If you can, imagine three hundred people crammed in here. You have to get them fitted with skates and get them out on the rink. You have a game every fifteen or twenty minutes. That's a big job, and you have to work fast. But I'm getting older now, and the last five years I've taken life a little easier. I have a manager, and I'm not here the many hours that I used to be. I just come in when I want to.

This roller rink is very well managed and well thought of. There are no bad things that happen here. I have enjoyed this business very much, and roller-skating around here is more popular than ever.

WANDA YOUNG,
ENCHANTED VALLEY INTERSKATE,
LEBANON, MISSOURI
POLLY BROWN

I was born and raised on the old highway here. I was five years old when Route 66 was built, and I can remember every bit of it. Pretty impressive to a little boy. Most of it was done with horses. There weren't any bulldozers or earth movers.

My dad said that Route 66 ruined his farm. He had bought three tracts of land over the years, and the road happened to go through every one of them. But it was a lot of entertainment for us kids because we hardly ever got to town. Around the highway, you could always see something going on right in our own backyard.

When the road first opened, there was just an occasional car. Maybe there was one every minute or so, except on holidays, when the two lanes would be full. One-hundredth of what it is now.

We used Route 66 as a playground at night. We were farm boys with not much to do. When a car was coming over the hill, we would take turns lying down on the highway. When the "dead man" was sure he had been seen by the car, he would jump up and dash for the woods. We were pretty ornery.

The trucks at that time were vastly underpowered. Many had only Model T or Model A motors. About halfway up Cooper Hill, just east of the farm, they would be in their lowest gear and moving at a crawl. My older brother and his friends would lie in wait for the trucks carrying watermelon. One or two boys would hop aboard and "harvest" a couple of melons and enjoy an evening snack.

ROBERT MAGNIN,
ST. JAMES, MISSOURI

JANE BERNARD

Dean Walker

WE ARRANGE TO MEET DEAN WALKER at the Eisler Brothers' store in Riverton, Kansas. Dean is an expert on the "Spooklight," a glowing, floating orb of greenish light that appears along the border of Missouri and Kansas.

The first thing he does is show us how he can turn his feet around 180 degrees backward. Dean seems to be an unusual guy, and a man of few words. He has brought along a buddy of his who drives a big black pickup truck with a toolbox in the back and the biggest antenna we've ever seen. The plan is that we are to follow them in our vehicle to a location where the Spooklight is known to appear.

We follow them down overgrown country roads, deeper and deeper into the heart of the rural backwoods. We try to make a mental note of the myriad turns we've taken, many of them unmarked. There is something a little spooky about the area.

Our conversation turns to "What if they ditch us here?" and, "Should we leave a trail of bread crumbs?" It eventually moves on to "Will we be sold into white slavery?"

Finally we stop on a nondescript, remote dirt road thick with vegetation. Dean shares his Spooklight stories with us, as well as wild tales of Witches' Holler. He uses wonderful words like "mysteryism" and tells us that no matter what people say, he believes the Spooklight is just swamp gas.

Dean and his friend turn out to be true gentlemen. After giving us a brief driving tour of Witches' Holler, they lead us back out to the main road.

Kansas

Stories about the "spooklight" go back as far as I can remember. Clear back to the Civil War. There are a lot of theories about what it is. Some people say it's little green men from Mars. There are people who say it's the gas refinery out of Copperville, Kansas. There are people who say that it's two Indians that jumped off Lover's Leap at Devil's Promenade Bridge who are trying to find their bodies. Then there's the story about a miner floating around out there, looking for his head. There's all kind of stuff out on it. But mostly, it's swamp gas.

The strange glowing ball remains one of the few things left on earth which defies all effort to strip it of its mysteryism.

Some say the spooklight has been here for more than eighty years. I first saw it in 1955. I was four years old. It was a light floating through the woods. I've seen it go through the driver's side of a

car window and float out. I've seen it on top of the car. I've seen it floating down the middle of the road. I've seen it bouncing around the trees. There are two roads down here that people have seen it on. One's the old road that Spooky Shack is on.

An old guy they called Mr. Spook used to live in a little old shack up here, about twelve feet square. He'd paint himself up like a skeleton, with aluminum fluorescent paint. Be as naked as a jaybird. He'd charge you $5 to watch him dance around inside his shack with a black light on him, like a skeleton.

You might go down there for one whole week, seven days and seven nights, and just sit and see nothing. Then you might go down there the following night, sit there for five minutes, and see the spooklight. But if you don't see it in twenty minutes, you aren't going to see it.

It's always been swamp gas.

DEAN WALKER,
SPOOKLIGHT EXPERT,
WITCHES' HOLLER, KANSAS
POLLY BROWN

This store is a kind of icon for the community, especially for folks that went to school here years ago. We just had Riverton High School's seventy-fifth anniversary. At the banquet, I asked how many people had worked at the store over the years. About thirty hands went up. For a lot of people, working at Eisler Brothers was their first job.

SCOTT NELSON, EISLER BROTHERS'
OLD RIVERTON STORE,
RIVERTON, KANSAS
JANE BERNARD

Harley and Annabelle

W E ARE DRIVING IN WESTERN OKLAHOMA and have only four more people to visit on this trip before we can head home. Two of them, Harley and Annabelle Russell, live in Erick, Oklahoma. We have heard that in their Sandhills Curiosity Shop they sing for their customers, and we have promised to drop by.

As we approach the shop, we notice a tour bus parked at the curb. As we enter, we are astonished by the amount of stuff packed inside the room. Every corner is crammed with curios, antiques, and musical instruments. Objects hang from the walls and the ceiling; more items sit in display cases and on top of them.

Approximately thirty senior citizens sit on folding chairs in the midst of the clutter. Facing them are Harley and Annabelle, wearing matching overalls with large red-and-white stripes. Harley is shirtless.

"Welcome to Erick, Oklahoma, the redneck capital of the world!" exclaims Harley. "We are the Mediocre Music Makers, and I'm an honest-to-goodness real redneck." At that, he takes a long swig from a bottle.

Harley and Annabelle sing "golden oldies" and Route 66 songs to their rapt audience. When they finish their gig forty-five minutes later, they serve sodas and sandwiches to the tourists. On each small table stands a glass cookie jar; these quickly fill up with dollar bills.

When the time comes for the bus to leave, Harley and Annabelle insist that we take a group photo of them with the whole tour. That done, they run outside and stand near the middle of the street waving a huge Route 66 sign as the tour bus pulls away.

Oklahoma

We spend the next couple of hours with them, sitting in their cluttered shop, as they tell us their life stories and Harley takes many more swigs from his bottle. We notice for the first time that there are no price tags on the items in the shop and that we haven't seen either Harley or Annabelle handle any money.

"Oh, we don't have time for that," Harley explains. "If someone wants something, they just take it and put what they want in those jars. We're far too busy playing music to bother with that."

HARLEY AND ANNABELLE RUSSELL,
THE MEDIOCRE MUSIC MAKERS,
THE SAND HILLS CURIOSITY SHOP, ERICK, OKLAHOMA
POLLY BROWN

HARLEY:

Annabelle and I call ourselves the Mediocre Music Makers, and we put on these shows for the tour buses and other tourists who travel Route 66. But it's quite a story how we got here.

I was born here on Route 66 in Erick, Oklahoma — the redneck capital of the world. I was in the music business for twenty-two years, and after going through five wives, I didn't have enough money to live anywhere else but here. I came back to my hometown, where I could live for nearly free. Fantastic!

ANNABELLE:

I'm the fifth wife. I'm number five.

HARLEY:

I wanted a fifth wife who would last forever, so I stopped with Annabelle. I was living here alone in this building, which was the original meat market in downtown Erick. One day I was sitting here in this wicker rocking chair — the same one that my granddad died in. This car pulled up, Annabelle and her mom got out, and I took one look at Annabelle and said to her, "Honey, you came to the right place." Anyway, we got to jamming and talking, and I told her to go home and pick up her stuff and come back. A month later, here she came. She came here from northern California, where the redwood trees are, and she's been here ever since.

ANNABELLE:

That's his story. My grandparents had a farm here. I used to come from California to stay with them every summer when I was a kid. I was here with my mother visiting my grandparents when I dropped my guitar and I couldn't get it back in tune. My mother brought me to Harley's place and, when we pulled up in front, Harley said to my mother, "Did you bring her here for me?" He tuned the guitar and, when my mother tried to pay him, he said, "I want to hear a song. That will be my payment." I played one song, and it was obvious I needed guitar lessons. Moving here from California was quite an adjustment. I'm still getting guitar lessons from Harley.

Ed Galloway built the multisided Fiddle House on the east side of his Totem Pole Park. It housed over three hundred fiddles that he hand-carved. His goal was to carve one fiddle from every kind of wood in the world.

Totem Pole Park is one of America's best-known examples of American folk art. The park contains several carved totem poles, including the world's largest, adorned with hundreds of figures. From the mid-1930s until his death in 1963, Galloway created an original monument to the American Indian.

In the late 1980s the Kansas Grassroots Art Association began the restoration of the park, and it was placed on the National Register of Historic Places in 1999.

THE FIDDLE HOUSE AND TOTEM POLE PARK,
FOYIL, OKLAHOMA

JANE BERNARD

THE Y BAR, COMMERCE, OKLAHOMA

POLLY BROWN

I was a teenager during the Dust Bowl era, and this gray dirt would blow in from Colorado. You'd see a big old bank coming up, and you couldn't tell if it was a cloud of rain or dust. Nine times out of ten it was dust, and the next day everything would be covered with gray dirt. It didn't rain here for years. Sometime in the 1930s it started raining again.

Once, when I was hitch-hiking, I caught a ride with a guy in a brand new 1936 Chevrolet, and he took me through places where the farmers had driven off and left their farms. The dust had drifted up around their abandoned houses and their equipment was sticking out through the dirt. During that time the loan companies had more farms then they wanted, and they couldn't sell them or rent them. We didn't have much food and we couldn't raise nothing. We'd plant food for our horses and it'd grow, but it wouldn't make grain.

After I returned from the war in 1947, I rented a farm from a woman whose husband had died in the 1930s. She tried to give her farm back to the loan company, but they wouldn't take it. She didn't want to just drive off and leave it. The Farmers Home Administration (FHA) talked her into hiring a supervisor. They loaned her money to pay for her farm, and it started paying off. By the time I rented from her, she had bought a home in Elk City and paid for it. The FHA and the WPA (Works Progress Administration), they were lifesavers for this country.

The way the war came along and bailed us out was kind of a miracle. We made war equipment for the whole world to fight with and sold it to other countries. Then, after the war, everybody needed everything. We had to sign up and wait eight months for a refrigerator.

BILL VARNER,
BILL'S BARBER SHOP,
CLINTON, OKLAHOMA

JANE BERNARD

Mr. George L. Coleman Sr. built this theater in 1929. He started out as a water-well driller and struck a very rich vein of lead and zinc. He acquired land and mineral rights and formed a mining company that turned out to be one of the richest fields in the world and continued to produce for decades. In the early 1920s and 1930s, Mr. Coleman was making almost a million dollars a month! To say he was a multimillionaire was conservative.

Mr. Coleman was a big fan of theater and vaudeville. He often traveled, both for business and pleasure, and would always go to the theater. One day he looked at an empty lot of his and decided to build his own theater. He called the Boller Brothers, architects from Kansas City who had built most of the big movie palaces around the country, and said, "I want this to be the most luxurious theater between Kansas City, Dallas, Denver, and St. Louis." The grand opening occurred on April 18, 1929.

We had Will Rogers perform here, as well as Tom Mix, the silent film Western movie star. Sally Rand performed here. Oh, my! She was a showstopper, literally a showstopper. Bing Crosby and Bob Hope and Groucho Marx all made appearances here in their vaudeville days. Older people swear they saw Al Jolson on this stage.

The Coleman was and is a social center for the community. In the 1930s, before World War II, the Coleman was actually the unofficial country club of the city. The real country club cost lots of money to belong to. At the Coleman, all you had to do was to buy a ticket. You could come and sit on the mezzanine and meet important people, famous people, and often very wealthy people. People came here to see and be seen.

Some of the older ladies that come through on our tours talk about how they came and bought tickets and never went to the show or the performance. They came to the mezzanine and visited. Young men did the same thing if they were looking for a wife.

If you had guests that came in, say, from Kansas City, this was the place to entertain them. You'd introduce them to the society editor, who was sitting on a divan. You'd tell the editor who you were, who your guests were, and what they were doing in town.

Then you would wait for the newspaper to be thrown in your yard the next day, and there it would be on the society page. The story would run something like: "Mr. and Mrs. Smith were seen entertaining guests from Kansas City at the Coleman Theater Friday night. Mrs. Smith was wearing the latest fall fashion from Milliner Burke," which was the upscale department store here. "Mrs. Smith's guest, Mrs. Jones, was wearing the latest fashion from Macy's of Kansas City." That's what all the women wanted to know.

The story would also mention the men. "Mr. Smith's guest, Mr. Jones, is rumored to be representing Eagle Pitcher Industries in opening a new mine in the Pitcher Field."

You would send your kid to the drug store to get ten more papers, and then you would cut the stories out and write letters to all your friends. Your friends would read the clippings and supposedly be suitably impressed. Then when they came to visit, they would expect you to bring them to the Coleman and introduce them to the society editor. It was an endless round.

LARRY IRWIN,
COLEMAN THEATER,
MIAMI, OKLAHOMA

JANE BERNARD

My family moved to Miami in the late 1950s. My memory of the Coleman is that it was like a palace. I guess it's why they call it a movie palace. I remember the luxurious thick carpets, and the wonderful royal burgundy color that was everywhere, and marbles and satins and silks. It's now completely stripped, compared to what it was.

Over time, many of the old theaters fell into disrepair, and the Coleman was no exception. The only thing that really saved this theater is that we are a small town and not a major city, where theaters have been torn down to make way for other types of development.

In 1989 the Coleman family decided to give the theater to the city of Miami, with the stipulation that the theater be restored to its original form, be a performing arts center, and be available to the schools. However, the family did not leave an endowment for us. Through the formation of the Friends of the Coleman and the Miami Downtown Redevelopment Authority, the city was able to keep the theater going and start a restoration process.

I grew up here, next door to the Round Barn. When I was little, there were places along the side of the barn wall that were busted out, and it was leaning and twisted to one side. There were telephone poles holding it up here and there. I used to have nightmares about that barn, and now I'm working here.

People come from all over to see the only round barn, which it ain't. I wish it were. Well, there's three hundred round barns on the east side of the United States alone but this is the only one on Route 66. The Shakers brought the idea over. They built the barn round for one reason, that way the devil couldn't corner you.

We have a gift shop and we rent out the upstairs for barn dances, weddings, family reunions, and parties. The only thing you can't have up there is a square dance. The barn's round!

ERNEST LEE "BUTCH" BREGER,
THE OLD ROUND BARN, ARCADIA, OKLAHOMA
POLLY BROWN

REST HAVEN MOTEL

AFTON, OKLAHOMA

JANE BERNARD

THE BLUE WHALE,

CATOOSA, OKLAHOMA

JANE BERNARD

Hugh Davis built the Blue Whale in the early 1970s as an anniversary gift for his wife, Zelta. It was originally intended only for family members but local kids kept sneaking in for a dip so the Davis family opened the swimming hole to the public. The park closed in 1988.

OKLAHOMA

POLLY BROWN

FOURTH OF JULY PARADE,
EDMOND, OKLAHOMA

JANE BERNARD

FOURTH OF JULY PARADE,
EDMOND, OKLAHOMA

POLLY BROWN

FOURTH OF JULY,

ELK CITY, OKLAHOMA

JANE BERNARD

METRO DINER,

TULSA, OKLAHOMA

JANE BERNARD

P.J.'S BAR-B-QUE

CHANDLER, OKLAHOMA

JANE BERNARD

LARRY SHAFER,

SPEED-A-WAY, MIAMI, OKLAHOMA

JANE BERNARD

OLD ROUTE 66, OKLAHOMA

JANE BERNARD

Cadillac Ranch

WE HAVE JUST LEFT AMARILLO, and our eyes scan the horizon to our left looking for Cadillac Ranch. Sunset, the magic hour for making images, is no more than an hour away. However, we're not hopeful since the sky is dark and ominous with thunderheads.

Suddenly the cars appear. From the road they look like miniature slanted pegs in the ground. They are placed in the middle of a recently plowed field about three hundred yards from the highway.

As we trudge out to the site, a light rain begins to fall. By the time we reach the Cadillacs, the drizzle has become a severe storm, complete with lightning, thunder and torrents of rain. We have no chance to take cover, and the angle of the cars is not quite steep enough to provide us with any shelter. At one point we find ourselves hugging the underbelly of a Cadillac, our camera bags at our bellies, trying to keep our equipment dry. It occurs to us that we are perfect targets for the lightning flashing around us.

In twenty minutes, the rain eases and the worst of the storm moves on. Finally we have our first close-up look at the cars. They are amazing, every one of them covered with bright graffiti. We try and walk around but wet, thick mud as deep as our ankles makes movement difficult. When we finally extract ourselves, we find our shoes are so mud-packed that they resemble huge moon boots and weigh a ton. We kick the Cadillacs repeatedly in a unsuccessful attempt to shake off the mud.

Just as we are about to lose all hope for any good images, the sky clears in the west, revealing a crimson sun at the horizon. There are only a few seconds of magical light, but they are enough.

Texas

CADILLAC RANCH,
AMARILLO, TEXAS

POLLY BROWN

When I moved off the ranch into Adrian in 1990 my daughter was in junior high and I decided I had to do something besides wander the streets of town. I'd never been involved in any kind of business venture before but I took over the café. At the time I didn't have much knowledge of Route 66 other than I had watched the old TV series. As my network grew I realized how very important these old places were and how important we were to Route 66.

Those of us who work along the road on a daily basis, we do get discouraged sometimes. We struggle to keep open. We're dependent on tourism, and our locals keep us going in the winter-time, in the hard months. But it's our foreign travelers and our Americans who are interested in Route 66 that really are the bulk of our business.

I cannot tell you how many times people have sat in these booths and looked out the window and said, "I remember being here as a seven-year-old, when my folks were going to California." That's pretty amazing to me that people made this trip so many times and they're just now rediscovering it.

FRAN HOUSER,

MIDPOINT CAFÉ, ADRIAN, TEXAS

POLLY BROWN

I've been a resident of Vega, Texas, since 1949, when I moved here with my husband. Vega, I love it! I've worn out a lot of shoes here. It's just a country town, but it has all the friends that you could want. I live at the end of Route 66 in Oldham County, and we claim that when you get to Oldham County, you're halfway down Route 66 from Chicago to Santa Monica.

My husband and I owned and operated Vega Zero Lockers for years. He butchered and did all the beef processing for the Panhandle. We stored meat for people, for that was the time before anyone had deep freezers in their homes. We sold ice to the tourists who came down Route 66.

I've had Dot's Mini Museum since 1990. It all started with an old cream separator, and I just kept adding antiques. Friends have given me a lot of antiques, but mostly it's just the things I have found at garage sales and saved. You'd be surprised what you can find at garage sales. I have quite a collection, for I was born and raised in the depression, and I never throw anything out.

One of my most prized possessions is a butter mold. I wanted my grandchildren to know what a butter mold was and how it was used. I now have fourteen grandchildren, thirty-five great-grandchildren, and one great-great-grandchild. That's five generations.

I love Route 66. I've been on the Mother Road for such a long time that it seems like home. It's kind of silly to like a highway so well, but I like Route 66, and I like everybody that likes Route 66.

DOT LEAVITT,
DOT'S MINI MUSEUM,
VEGA, TEXAS

JANE BERNARD

For forty years I worked for the railroad in five states — Missouri, Arkansas, Oklahoma, Texas and New Mexico.

Then, in 1982, I started raising bees. That first year, I had ten hives and sold about $400 worth of honey. Now I have seventy-two hives, and I get about seven fifty-five-gallon barrels of honey.

We raise our own bees, and we raise our own queens. Right now we're running Russian bees. They try better. They will get up and go to work when the temperature is forty degrees, and most bees won't get up and work until it is sixty-six degrees.

We sell bees, honey, bee pollen, and propolis. Propolis is that gummy, sticky stuff that bees produce. It's an antibiotic, and people buy it for health reasons because they want to live longer. We sell to grocery stores, fruit markets, restaurants, and local areas here in the Panhandle and New Mexico. We ship quite a bit all over the country.

I don't sell as much honey commercially as I did once. They wanted me to put bar codes on the labels, and I wouldn't do that. I'm a Christian, have been one all my life, and those bar codes go against my beliefs. They have the sign of the beast on them.

I don't need to sell my honey to the stores because I have my customers out there waiting for the honey crop. They know and I know that it's 100 percent honey. Government honey, you don't know what's in it.

LOREN JONES,

JONES HONEY AND BEE APIARY,

LELA, TEXAS

JANE BERNARD

REMAINS OF THE LITTLE JUAREZ DINER,

GLENRIO, TEXAS—NEW MEXICO BORDER

JANE BERNARD

THE BIG TEXAN STEAK RANCH,

AMARILLO, TEXAS

POLLY BROWN

BOBBY:

There are eight of us kids, five brothers and three sisters. Danny and I are both up toward the top of the food chain.

Our world rotated inside the sphere of the Big Texan when we were growing up. There were two playpens in the kitchen. One of them was for the little bitty babies and the other was for the toddlers. The older kids, like Danny, me, and Diane, would stand on crates that put us at worktable level. My dad's chef would give us onions to prep or chickens to chop up or shrimp to peel. When we got out of school, we would go right to the accountant's office to do our homework and then to the kitchen.

DANNY:

Sometimes Bob and I wonder why my dad had eight kids. Was it for the cheap labor or did he have the restaurant to feed all of us?

BOBBY:

My dad was a Yankee from the North who had never been to Texas. When he got to the Panhandle, he wondered, "Where are the cowboys?" So he had this idea of what he saw in the movies about an old western–looking place. In 1960, he built almost a Yankee-style barbecue place with a little western theme.

It really was by accident that he discovered the power of the cowboy. The original place on Route 66 was not far from the Amarillo stockyard. When the cowboys would get off work, they'd show up at the restaurant. People would just sit around and eye-gog at them.

He started cashing the cowboys' paychecks on Friday and served them twenty-five-cent beers. These guys would end up spending half their paychecks before they'd even left the place.

One of these cowboys had a horse in his trailer that got out one Friday night in the parking lot. That cowboy ran out there and jumped on that horse and got him under control. There were people running into each other on Route 66, pulling off the road with their cameras. My dad looked out there and it was incredible, the sensation this thing caused. So he got a cowboy and said, "Look, you come back tomorrow. I'll pay you twenty-five bucks to just sit on your horse and wave to people." The guy thought he was crazy.

People started pouring in off the highway to see this cowboy. From there on out, my dad dressed his employees as cowboys and had them carry little six-guns at their sides. Then up went the cowboy sign and the magic happened from that point, right then and there.

DANNY:

The cowboys from the stockyard always caused a stir in the place. They were such pigs when they ate. My dad was always amazed at how much they could put away. So he said, "I'll tell you what. Next Friday night, when you guys get paid, everybody come up here and put up $5. I'm going to serve you one-pound steaks for one hour, and whoever eats the most gets all the money in the pot." Then my dad called the media and did whatever he could do to get people in the place. There was a buzz about it all over town. Even local people were interested in knowing about this.

Sure enough, the cowboys showed up and my dad started serving them one-pound steaks for an hour. One guy was ahead of everybody, and he said, "Well, bring me a salad, too. What else you got there? Bring me a shrimp cocktail and bring me a roll." By the time the hour was up, this cowboy had eaten four-and-a-half pounds of steak, the shrimp cocktail, a salad, and a piece of bread. My dad declared him the winner and said, "From this day forward, anybody that comes in here and eats a seventy-two-ounce steak, complete with side orders, will get it for free." And lo and behold, that's how it all started.

BOBBY AND DANNY LEE,
THE BIG TEXAN STEAK RANCH,
AMARILLO, TEXAS
POLLY BROWN

MCLEAN, TEXAS

JANE BERNARD

The cross was designed, funded, and built by Texas engineer Steve Thomas. Completed in 1993, it is the largest cross in the Western Hemisphere, rising nineteen stories high with an arm span of one hundred ten feet.

EAST OF MCLEAN, TEXAS

POLLY BROWN

Stanley Marsh III, a ranching and broadcasting scion and avid art collector from Amarillo, loved the old highway and believed that if you can afford it, life should be like a circus. In 1974 Marsh collaborated with members of the Ant Farm, a group of experimental architects, to design some art that represents the American dream.

Together they created Cadillac Ranch. It was important to Marsh that folks on the highway realize the Cadillacs had been planted there by members of a highly intelligent civilization. That's why he had them grounded in concrete, tail fins up, at the exact angles of the Great Pyramid.

Marsh viewed Cadillac Ranch as a celebration of the American dream and believed it to be the "Stonehenge of America."

CADILLAC RANCH, AMARILLO, TEXAS

JANE BERNARD

GROOM, TEXAS

POLLY BROWN

DOT'S MINI MUSEUM,
VEGA, TEXAS

POLLY BROWN

The Aztec Motel

IT'S EARLY ON A SUMMER EVENING as we drive east on Albuquerque's Central Avenue, headed toward the Aztec Motel. We called earlier to secure an appointment with the owner, Mohammed Natha. His wife told us not to come before 6 P.M. because Mohammed naps in the afternoon.

The Aztec is hard to miss. It stands out in this neighborhood of cheap motels and eateries as if dressed in a fancy costume. The low evening light shines on the side of the motel, highlighting walls that are covered with pictures, flags, garlands, and tinsel. The roof is crowded with figurines, dolls, mannequins, toy trucks, and trains. On the ground around the periphery of the motel sit old wine and whiskey bottles filled with plastic and silk flowers.

Mohammed beckons us into his office, which also serves as his living room. "Are you hungry? Are you thirsty?" he asks. "We have a chicken ready for you, and you must have some wine. Or maybe you would prefer a beer?" We try and refuse, but he insists. "No interview, no photos unless you eat and drink." So we eat and drink, fearful that we will lose the light before we can photograph or be incapable of conducting an interview after drinking the wine.

Phyllis bursts into the room and greets us with enthusiasm. Phyllis Evans is a retired university professor who has lived at the Aztec for years and is responsible for all the motel's decorations. She tells us how she combs local thrift stores looking for interesting

New Mexico

objects, and how she gives the winos on Central change for their empty bottles. It's obvious that she thinks of the Aztec as her own home, and, in fact, she has become something akin to a co-manager with Mohammed. He believes she has been the savior of the motel.

The small office/living room is certainly the motel's hub. The Aztec has only long-term guests, and this evening they wander in and out, asking Mohamed for something they need or sometimes just asking advice about a family or money issue. Mohammed is the patriarch and the guests are his extended family.

Mohammed and Phyllis banter back and forth like the best friends they are. Somehow we conduct an interview with both of them and take some photographs before the last light disappears. It is time to leave, but Mohammed wants us to have more to eat and drink. We feel that if he had a vacant room in the motel he would ask us to stay, and we know that if we have any more of his wine we will have to.

MOHAMMED NATHA AND PHYLLIS EVANS,
AZTEC MOTEL, ALBUQUERQUE, NEW MEXICO
POLLY BROWN

MOHAMMED NATHA:

I was born in Zanzibar in East Africa in 1946. My parents were born in India. I came to America in 1985. I acquired the Aztec Motel in June 1991. So from then on we have run our ship with our own rules, just like the *Titanic*.

We have our rules on our ship, and if anybody doesn't like our rules, they can just look for another ship. We don't like our *Titanic* to sink. No troublemakers, no visitors after 8 P.M. and no wild parties after 8 P.M. period. There are too many drug dealers, there are too many prostitutes, and there are too many gangster problems on Central Avenue in Albuquerque.

When I first saw this place, it was like a ghost town left on a dirt road. That's what it was. The parking lot wasn't paved and the rooms were all filthy.

On my first day here as owner, I saw car after car come through in one night. And I thought, "What the hell is happening over here?" So the next morning, I went to talk to the police sergeant, who told me they were planning on shutting the place down in another two or three days.

I had made a down payment of $10,000. When I decided to buy it, I didn't know there was this kind of traffic coming and going. So I asked the police officer for help. He gave me a real good boost. In fourteen days, he got rid of all the troublemakers.

The first year, the insurance people did not allow me to buy insurance. They said, "Sorry, this is a third-class place. This is kind of a 'Little Whorehouse in Albuquerque.'"

It took almost fourteen months to get things in shape. I repaired each of the rooms, one at a time. The $32,000 I brought with me just went like hotcakes. The parking lot cost me $8,000 to fix up. It took me $15,000 to fix up the roof. So all that money was gone.

Oh, my first two years were very tough. Then Phyllis showed up. It was as if the gods had sent me Mother Theresa. She helped me to create this place. All the pictures, the decorations on the walls, the landscaping and everything, those were her ideas. She is always creating, and she spends her own money to do these things. Anybody messing around with Phyllis over here can hit the road! She is the mother of our empire. I'm the owner of the ship, and she is the captain of the ship.

We have a kind of family environment here. When people see what a peaceful place we have, they stay for weeks and weeks and months and months. Just like Phyllis. She stayed for the first day, then she stayed for a week, and then she came in and asked me if she could pay for a year. She's been here now for eight years.

Every weekend, on Saturday and Sunday, we have a free meal for our tenants, about thirty-five people. I do the cooking, Phyllis does the dessert. We feed everybody. Phyllis and I are keeping this place as clean as a fresh flower and fit as a fiddle.

For the last ten years, we have complained about this area to the city people. Johns pick up prostitutes and drug dealers walk the streets here. They blame the motel people. But it is not our fault. We did not bring any prostitutes or drug dealers from where we came from, Africa or India or wherever. What are we supposed to do? We can't take the law into our hands and break their heads or something. And when we call the cops, the cops pick them up, they make a phone call, and their backup comes and bails them out.

I'll tell you the good thing about having the hotel. You run your business over here, you cook here, you eat here, you sleep here, you enjoy the TV. Everything is in one place.

You see, it's not going to give me enough money to be a "thousandaire" or a millionaire, but at least it's hand to mouth. You have to be a satisfied person in your life. I have enjoyed my life and I feel like God has given me happy satisfaction. Whenever I want to drink a beer, I drink a beer. Whenever we want to eat a chicken, we eat a chicken. Whenever we want to go to the casino, Phyllis and I can just go and spend $15 or $50 dollars, just go and enjoy. What we should say is that Phyllis and I and my family are going the way the flow wants to go.

There should be only one principle in your life: Be good to human beings. Then you can expect good deeds out of other people. If you are a bad guy, don't expect to get any good news. You always have to put your heart with people and make them feel that they are treated as family members. That is what they love.

PHYLLIS EVANS:

I was trying to find a place to live and got the idea of moving into a motel. I hadn't the slightest idea of what I was getting into. When I met Mohammed, I thought, "What a fun guy, and what a wonderful thing he is trying to do here." All these people were saying to me, "I can't believe you live at the Aztec." Everybody was quite horrified because this place had the worst reputation of any motel in Albuquerque.

They treat me like family here. I broke my leg and had to have reconstructive surgery. Mohammed said, "We'll take care of you." I'm sure that the people here did a much better job of it than an institution would have. I have assisted living, only it isn't institutionalized; it's done with love.

I graduated from high school in 1954, and times were so bad I spent a whole year looking for a job. The only work I could get was picking blue corn for sixty-five cents an hour. I had to pay the recruiter fifty cents for the ride, a dollar for gloves, and a dollar for a sandwich. A girl invited me to her prom and by the time I bought her corsage, I was in the hole.

I had a relative who knew I had some art ability, and he suggested I go see Jim Hall at Ace Neon Sign Company. I didn't even know that people made a living painting signs, and I didn't know what neon was. I thought all I needed was a few brushes and some paint and I could be a sign painter. Boy, was I naïve. Jim Hall said to me, "Son, you haven't lived long enough to be a sign painter. This is an education, just like going to college. It will take you five years of apprenticeship."

So I went to work for nothing, just to learn the trade. I learned fast, and at the end of every week Jim would hand me a $5 bill because I think he believed in me. At that time, Hispanics weren't hired for anything. Jim Hall was kind of ostracized by the Anglo community. They would say, "Why did you hire that Mexican kid when there are so many Anglo kids who could use a job?" He told them he had tried the Anglo kids and they didn't last a week and that I had the guts to stick to it. So he gave me a break, and for that I was very grateful.

In 1955 Jim Hall retired, sold his business, and I moved to Albuquerque. That period was the heyday for Route 66 and for sign painters. We were painting for our customers, but the other sign painters were our critics. You could recognize another guy's signs, just like his handwriting.

RUDY GONZALES,

SIGNS BY RUDY, TUCUMCARI, NEW MEXICO

POLLY BROWN

I was born in Tucumcari and my family moved to California in 1954. We headed west like many families did at that time. I came back every summer to visit my cousins.

My aunt and uncle had owned the business for many years. They purchased it and ran it back when it made money. When we took it over, we were still witnessing the death of Old Route 66. There were probably five or six stores like ours in this area, and, one by one, they closed up shop.

As an adult, I remembered Tucumcari through a child's eyes. When I was growing up, we didn't lock our doors, everybody was friendly, and I had a lot of cousins to run with. Those were some of the greatest days of my life. I envisioned bringing my kids back to all of that. In southern California there was a lot of drugs and violence. Well, you can never get away from drugs, there is a lot less violence in this community. However, it isn't the ideal place that I remembered from my childhood.

A while back we had some college kids that came through and they were writing papers on *The Grapes of Wrath*. Maybe I looked old to them because my beard's gone white, but I'm not that old. They came in and asked me if I'd owned the business during the Dust Bowl era. If they're gonna be that stupid, you know, they deserve what they get. I unloaded a great story with all the trimmings about how we felt so bad for the people traveling through that we would stand out in the evenings and hand out cheese and pimento sandwiches as the old cars drove through with families on board. Of course, I wasn't even born then, but what the heck.

MIKE CALLENS,
TEE PEE CURIOS,
TUCUMCARI, NEW MEXICO

JANE BERNARD

CHRISTINA CAMPOS,

MANAGER OF JOSEPH'S RESTAURANT, SANTA ROSA, NEW MEXICO

JOSEPH CAMPOS, MAYOR OF SANTA ROSA AND STATE REPRESENTATIVE

POLLY BROWN

JOSEPH:

The heyday of Route 66 was an exciting time. It's amazing how the road is such an icon in the American mind. It's Elvis Presley and Buddy Holly. It's about America. The story of Route 66 is really the story of the United States becoming mobile and finding new opportunities. It's the story, too, of the beginning of the scattering of families. Before they could travel, families stayed in one area from generation to generation. With the establishment of Route 66, individuals could move away to a new area where they had no relatives. Is that a good thing? I don't know. Route 66 was a part of people disconnecting from their roots, and that was a big change.

In 1956 my parents opened up a restaurant, really just a drive-in, here in Santa Rosa. In 1963 they turned it into a cafeteria. Then, all of a sudden, when the interstate came through, this part of town just died. Shortly thereafter, the oil crisis hit. It was like a one-two punch. It knocked us down.

A lot of people sold out for whatever they could get and moved away. Many sold out to an employee or to anybody who was willing to buy. They even carried the notes. It gave a few people opportunities to buy a business.

I got married in 1985. It was a cold and cloudy day when we drove through town for the first time together. The roads were empty, and as we passed by the downtown area, tumbleweeds were rolling down Main Street just like in the movie *The Last Picture Show*. I could envision the scene in black and white. My wife started crying. She is from Albuquerque. Big-town girl coming to a small town. And she was saying, "This is home?"

I came back here to help my dad out because he helped me out through college. My wife and I didn't intend to stay. I promised my dad I'd be here for two years, and then we were going back to Albuquerque. After we had our first child, we realized we wanted to raise our kids here.

Santa Rosa became our home. We've seen a lot of improvement to the community. Now there is traffic downtown. In fact, last year we didn't see one boarded-up storefront anywhere. Just seven, eight years ago, almost all of them were boarded up.

We used to have lots of people here who tried to make a living in the service industries. People would often be able to buy cars and houses in the summer but then lose them in the winter when business was slow, and they couldn't make the payments. Now, with at least one family member working in the schools, for the state, or for the correctional facility, people have some stability in their income level. This has helped create an economic foundation and a new optimism for our community.

CHRISTINA:

After Joseph and I were married, we came here in the winter, and it was desolate. I had grown up in Albuquerque, where the city just doesn't shut down like that. I had no friends or family here. I had this feeling of loneliness and of not belonging.

We came to help Joseph's father with the restaurant. I thought I would have some time to kick back, but within a few days I had to start working. I started out as the cashier. Joseph was cook and waiter. Little by little I took over the books.

We had decided to put off having children for five years, but in three weeks I discovered that I was pregnant. By spring, when I had the baby, I felt at home in the community. Joseph's friends had become my friends. All the people in this town are so supportive. I don't have family here by blood, but I've made my own family.

I left the restaurant for three years and became the chief finance officer at the hospital. I was able to create my own identity separate from Joseph's world.

When I came back to the restaurant I enjoyed it so much more. When I first worked there, I was so young, only twenty, and I wasn't respected by the employees. When I returned, I carried my success at the hospital with me.

This community has been really good to us, and it's been a wonderful place to raise our kids. I can take the children to the cemetery and they can see the stones of Joseph's father, his grandfather, and his great-grandfather.

I tell Joseph that if we ever get divorced, he will have to be the one to leave town. Santa Rosa has become my town. I'm a transplant, but my roots are in Santa Rosa now.

EARL'S FAMILY RESTAURANT,

GALLUP, NEW MEXICO

POLLY BROWN

MATTIE AND BILL RICHARDSON,

RICHARDSON'S TRADING POST,

GALLUP, NEW MEXICO

POLLY BROWN

My dad was a schoolteacher down near Fort Worth, Texas, and he and his brothers formed what they called the Richardson Brothers' Trading Company around 1913. They bought a wholesale house and started operating in several locations on the Navajo Reservation. In those days they were mostly just buying wool, sheep, cattle, and rugs. There was no money exchanged. When the Navajos came to the trading post they had sheep or wool that they sold in exchange for a trade slip, which they could in turn exchange for goods like flour, sugar, coffee, and shirts. They didn't have cash.

In those days there were very few tourists. Visitors would stay at the trading posts if there was room. They'd throw a Navajo blanket on the floor or counter to use as a bed. The trader was usually lonesome and wanted some company.

We left the reservation because the tribes wanted Indians running those stores, and the rules and regulations on the reservation were getting steeper. My mother opened a store here in Gallup in 1935, and in 1938 I started a little store of my own.

If you come in here the first of the month, you'll see this place packed with Indians. We do a big business in pawn. In the early days, they'd pawn a string of beads or a belt to get flour, sugar, coffee, canned peaches, or tomatoes, and they would leave their pawn in here until they sheared their sheep or brought in a rug.

When they come in today, they're buying automobiles, they've got to have insurance, maybe they want to take their kids to Disneyland. If they borrow $1,000, I charge them $100 the first month, and after that it drops down to $20 a month. We don't sell any pawn unless it's been here at least a year. We've got stuff that has been here ten years. The people who pawned it are either out of work or dead, and their kids or grandkids are the ones who will have to pay to get it back. We'll hold it until they get the money together. If I sell it, then they won't have it anymore.

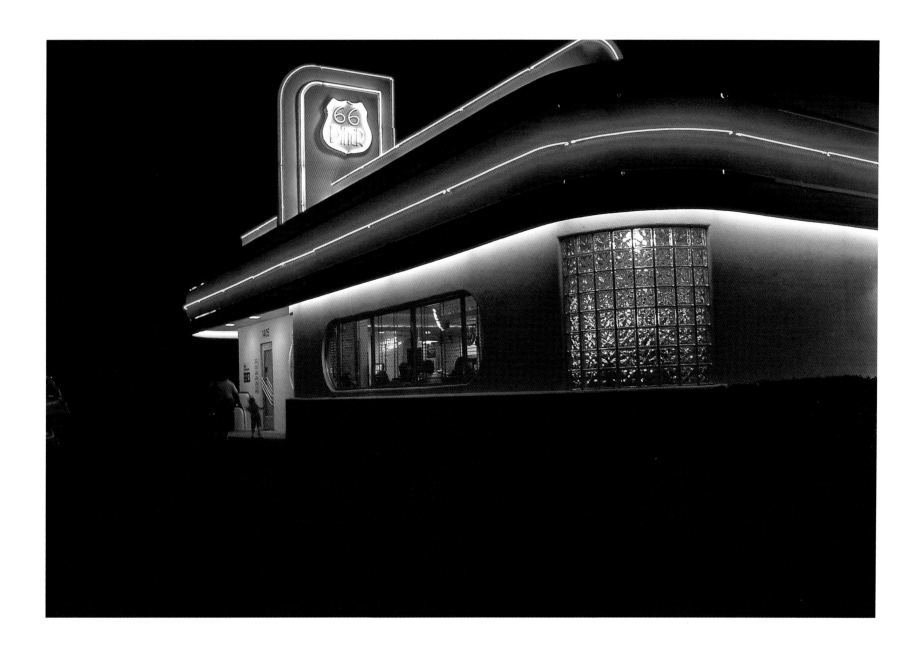

ROUTE 66 DINER,

ALBUQUERQUE, NEW MEXICO

POLLY BROWN

NIGHTLIFE,
ALBUQUERQUE, NEW MEXICO

JANE BERNARD

I opened my auto parts store September 12, 1959. This community's gone down considerably since the highway was moved. I'd venture to say we only have about seven gasoline stations to service the interstate. During the golden era, why, we had thirty-five or forty stations, and every one of them made a living.

During the depression, the government set up soup kitchens in various communities. Maybe you've read about it. Oh, that was pitiful at that time. They had one in Tucumcari, and they had one in Carrizozo. Many of the people who were going across the country in that day and age, many of them, I would say, were really desperate.

I worked at a filling station back then and would see these poor people headed for California. I recall seeing a man pushing a wheelbarrow with all the family possessions piled on top, with the wife and kids following behind.

I had a hard time making it, but I got through all right. Then the rumors of the war started, and things slowly began to improve.

During the war, we paid for things with ration coupons. Things were great then. Soldiers would come by and give you a few extra coupons. In that day and age, that was against the law. It's been over fifty years since then, so they can't do anything to me now.

Some places, why, they took advantage of people. One gimmick they had was to build a trough. The thing was pretty long, filled up with water, and they put up a sign: "Drive Through and Cool Your Tires, Fifty Cents."

ADOLPH SERRANO,

OWNER, CHIEF'S AUTO PARTS,

SANTA ROSA, NEW MEXICO

POLLY BROWN

My family originally came out here in 1928 to homestead from Cordell, Oklahoma. We traveled Route 66 in a covered wagon and the trip took thirty-one days. I was thirteen years old and really enjoyed it. I picked up pop bottles along the way. When I got out here, I sold them for two cents each to a guy who made whiskey. I sold enough to get me a cowboy hat and a few more clothes.

There weren't many travelers on Route 66 at the time, just some cars and a few covered wagons. It was in 1929 and 1930, when the Dust Bowl came on, that people really started going to California.

We came out here so my dad could own his own land. He was a farmer and he was used to living year to year. Back then we didn't know homesteading was hard because everybody was in the same boat. My dad bought a milk cow so we would have milk and butter. We had chickens, hogs, and we raised a lot of garden stuff.

TOM LAMANCE,
SWAP MEET 66,
BLUEWATER, NEW MEXICO

POLLY BROWN

specialize in selling the right kind of hat for the right occasion. I am also a milliner, and I can match the hat not only to the item but also to the person.

The revitalization of the Nob Hill area really took off probably fifteen years ago. What really spurred it was a group of people who came to New Mexico from other places and wanted to settle in a pedestrian historical area. They were creative and community minded. Most of the storeowners around here have known each other for some time. We all began opening our business about twenty years ago.

This type of neighborhood is becoming endangered. For every cut you make in the sidewalk for a driveway it becomes less pedestrian friendly. Once you get away from old Route 66 you start to lose a historical perspective. Albuquerque has grown like ripples from a stone dropped in water, and the outer reaches have no connection to the inner ring.

LARRY KOCH,

LARRY'S HATS, ALBUQUERQUE, NEW MEXICO

JANE BERNARD

NEW MEXICO STATE FAIR,
ALBUQUERQUE, NEW MEXICO

POLLY BROWN

GEORGE:

Route 66 went through Laguna, right there up the hill. It had a post office, grocery store, and a gas station. The gas station had those glass gas pumps that held ten gallons. At that time it was just regular gas: no ethyl, no unleaded. If you had enough money, you could get ten gallons, and at that time ten gallons could really fill up your tank.

There wasn't much traffic except during the summertime, when travelers came through on Old Route 66. Then there were buses: you know, Greyhound and Trailways. A lot of people didn't have vehicles then.

The old people would sell pins, pottery, and whatever else they could. They'd have a shed for shade and they'd take their lunch with them, and tourists would pull off the road and stop. Some of the old people spoke very broken English, and they didn't know how to count very well. If a piece of pottery cost $1, they would use their fingers and say, "Ten cents, ten cents, ten cents" ten times to count to a dollar.

I met my wife when I was driving a school bus. She was still in high school and I was her bus driver. I would pick up the students from all the villages of Laguna and take them to school in Grants. After we were married, I worked at the Anaconda Copper mine until it shut down in 1982.

MARY:

I used to sell pottery with my grandmother. She taught me how to make pots, and I used to help her out. She would gather her own clay and mix it herself. Everything we sold, she'd go half-and-half with me. I loved that time with her, and I wish she were alive today.

When my grandmother became too old to work, I sold pottery at a stand by myself. That lasted only two or three years. When the interstate came through, everybody quit because we weren't allowed to sell on the road anymore.

GEORGE AND MARY LUCERO,
MESITA VILLAGE,
LAGUNA PUEBLO, NEW MEXICO

JANE BERNARD

When I was in high school, I used to work in the gift shop, and a lot of times I was host. People would come in at that time and ask strange questions like "Is it necessary to roll up my windows when I go onto the reservation?" They really thought they would get arrows coming in through their car windows. Or they would ask, "Are white people allowed on the reservation?" It was really crazy, you know, the trepidation they felt about visiting the reservation. They really had no idea that Native Americans were just like them.

JOHN MARBURY,

GENERAL MANAGER, THE RANCH

KITCHEN, GALLUP, NEW MEXICO

POLLY BROWN

As a kid, I was voted school clown, a fun bozo. And the nickname stuck. About twenty-five years ago, I opened my shop. I was going to call it "Jim's Automotive," but then I thought, who in the hell is Jim? Nobody knew Jim. People know Bozo. That name and that shop have made me a lot of money.

People never forget that name—Bozo's. A lot of people come up to me and say, "I don't want no bozo working on my car." Then after they see what we do, hey, then they say, "You're the man!"

I love what I do, working with people, helping people. People break down here and they don't have any money to pay for their car repairs, and I let them ride right out of here. I don't worry about it. If you got the money, send it to me. If not, then it's a donation. And God's been good to me.

I had an aneurysm go off in my head in 1999. It's a miracle I'm still alive. I tell everybody that God didn't take me because I was on a mission to finish the Route 66 Auto Museum.

After I got out of the hospital, my wife handed me the deed to the property for our museum. She went out and bought it on her own, $75,000 for the three acres. She said, "Now, you figure out how to put your museum together." It tickled me to death.

There were people who wanted to chip in money to be part of the museum, and I said no. This way, if it doesn't go, I don't have to answer to nobody. Just to Bozo and my wife. All of us will eat cake by ourselves if it's successful, and if it's not, we'll eat the crumbs.

JAMES ("BOZO") CORDOVA,
BOZO'S GARAGE AND WRECKER SERVICE AND
BODY SHOP; OWNER, ROUTE 66 AUTO MUSEUM,
SANTA ROSA, NEW MEXICO

JANE BERNARD

SWAP MEET 66,

BLUEWATER, NEW MEXICO

POLLY BROWN

RANCH KITCHEN,

GALLUP, NEW MEXICO

JANE BERNARD

THE WHITING BROTHERS SERVICE STATION,
SAN FIDEL, NEW MEXICO

POLLY BROWN

Whiting Brothers was a small, regional, independent chain of gas stations started by Eddie, Ernest, Ralph, and Arthur Whiting in 1917. They erected what may have been the longest billboards that existed along old Route 66 and marketed themselves as offering "Gas for Less" and "Save Five Cents." The stations were spread throughout western states along Route 66, but the opening of the interstate doomed their bypassed locations.

SANTA ROSA, NEW MEXICO

JANE BERNARD

BLUE SWALLOW MOTEL,

TUCUMCARI, NEW MEXICO

JANE BERNARD

Floyd Redman gave his fiancée, Lillian, the Blue Swallow as a wedding present. She added the famous giant sign, which turned the Blue Swallow Motel into a Route 66 icon. Lillian ran the motel for forty years and by doing so helped keep Tucumcari on the map.

SANTA ROSA, NEW MEXICO

JANE BERNARD

Twin Arrows

THIS IS OUR THIRD TRIP TO ARIZONA since we began our Route 66 quest. There are less than 150 miles between the New Mexico border and Flagstaff, Arizona, but for the last two days it feels as if we have been back and forth across this same stretch of highway entirely too many times chasing that elusive magic light and getting the interviews and photographs that we need.

We have already had a busy day with photos and interviews in Adamana, Holbrook, and Winslow. Now it is afternoon and we are headed east once more. Our goal is to photograph at Twin Arrows, now a deserted truck stop and trading post but once a Route 66 icon. We have been there before but never at the right time of day for good light. This afternoon we've timed it right, and we should arrive at Twin Arrows just before sunset. But first we must stop at the Jack Rabbit Trading Post to photograph the famous "HERE IT IS" sign. The light is good, and if we are lucky a train will speed by the sign.

At Jackrabbit, there are bikers speaking a language we don't understand. It turns out they are eight Norwegians traveling all of Route 66 on rented Harley-Davidsons. They have T-shirts that say "Route 66 Norway Men's Tour" with the Norwegian flag printed on the front.

We photograph them, hear stories of their Route 66 adventure, and completely lose track of time. Now it is late and we still have miles to go before reaching Twin Arrows. We must jump on the interstate if we expect to have any light at all when we get there.

Arizona

We arrive as the last bit of light is disappearing behind San Francisco Peak. Truckers and motorists still pull over here to rest, even though the facilities are long gone. To our dismay, decomposing trash is strewn everywhere and the place smells like a dumpster. The arrows themselves look shabby, with paint peeling from them. After all of our efforts to get here, planning our day for this photo and risking speeding citations on I-40, we are sad and disappointed.

Of course, we still photograph. In the almost total darkness, we can only capture an image of the arrows silhouetted against the fading afterglow. We realize that the picture, shot this way, will show none of the discarded beer cans and other debris that's scattered about. The arrows will not reveal their peeling paint. Strangely enough, they will appear as they did decades ago, when Twin Arrows Trading Post and Truck Stop was a thriving business and a famous Route 66 landmark.

TWIN ARROWS, ARIZONA

POLLY BROWN

DINOS IN THE DESERT,

HOLBROOK, ARIZONA

JANE BERNARD

STEWART'S PETRIFIED WOOD,
ADAMANA, ARIZONA

JANE BERNARD

CHARLES AND GAZELL STEWART,

STEWART'S PETRIFIED WOOD,

ADAMANA, ARIZONA

POLLY BROWN

CHARLES:

My wife allows me to pitch in because she knows I am good at business. I did well when I worked in Phoenix selling TVs and appliances. I offered day-and-night service, weekend service, and free loaners for TVs and refrigerators. I knew as a black man I had to struggle to be successful, so I offered services that no one else did.

I always figured you could make it in this business if you could draw people off the road. To do that, you need to have something big and visible. We have billboards from Winslow to Gallup that say "Dinosaur Park: Enter Free at Stewart's" in four-foot letters. When they get close to our place, the families with children pull off because of our huge dinosaur sculptures. I make them so you can't miss them. I lie awake at night thinking up new things. I'm in the process of making this dinosaur with a long neck whose head will go up and down. I just put a new red tongue on that old dinosaur, and now you can see it much better from the road.

I consider us to be doing well. We'd make more money if I'd stop making so many dinosaurs.

GAZELL:

We once had Jerry Seinfeld here. He came in with his bodyguard, who was a little bitty man. He carried such a huge gun that he could hardly keep his pants up. The bodyguard picked up this $3,000 meteorite and was going to take it to their car. I told him he could not take it without paying for it first. Jerry tried to use his credit card, but it didn't work because the power was down. So I trusted him and let him have it anyway.

've been in business since 1976. I started the store when I was twenty-eight with $1,000. I just laugh that we survived for fifteen years on old Route 66 located next to Club 66, the most notorious Indian bar in the Southwest. I used to sweep out the Thunderbird bottles from my front alcove in the morning, and drunks would often sleep in my doorway at night.

We sell authentic Southwest American Indian art. We specialize in Hopi old-style kachina dolls and arts, crafts, and jewelry from Navajo and Hopi artists. We carry a few Pueblo artists as well. Everything in here is handmade, not mass-produced. We sell traditional Southwest herbs. I am an ethnobotanist, and I'm also the founder and director of the Arizona Ethnobotanical Research Association. My daughters are second-generation herbalists and traders. We really love it.

Before the road was Route 66, it was called Front Street. I liked that: It sounded like an old Wild West name. I could open my store anytime of the day or night and have customers come in off old Route 66. We were directly across from the train station, too. I lived behind my shop and had a wood-burning stove that was my only source of heat.

We are known as an Indian store because of our traditional herbs. The Native Americans are the ones who support my store and, of course, the tourists. We are unique and original, and now we get even more tourists. We're now located around the corner from my old shop on Route 66, and we're in the old, historic Babbitt Building.

PHYLLIS HOGAN,
ETHNOBOTANIST,
WINTER SUN TRADING COMPANY,
FLAGSTAFF, ARIZONA

JANE BERNARD

THE REVEREND UNCLE CHARLIE HICKS,

GHOSTRIDER GUNFIGHTER,

OATMAN, ARIZONA

POLLY BROWN

I would like to think that the gunfighters have put Oatman on the map. The wild burros that roam the streets are the town's main attraction, but the gunfights are the next most important draw. If on a particular day we don't put on a gunfight, people can get real upset. "I brought so-and-so all the way from England to see a gunfight, and you're not doing it?" I'm bragging now, but yes, the Ghostrider Gunfighters have done wonders to get people to come to Oatman.

We put on our gunfight shows seven to nine times a week. After we finish our show, we pick ourselves up off the pavement and take up a collection by passing our hats around, and that is how we raise money for charity.

We finally were incorporated as a nonprofit in 1995, and I'm proud to say that we have raised $25,000 for the Shriners' Children's Hospital burn centers. We've been able to give $7,000 to the Oatman Chamber of Commerce, and we've helped numerous people in distress, folks who maybe had their house burn down or were going through some bad times. The only person we have on the payroll is the man we have loading our ammunition. The rest of us are volunteers.

We have about thirty different shows that we put on. We have eight gunfighters, but right now we're shorthanded. We sometimes block off the street and put on a shotgun wedding. This guy is trying to back out of getting married, but the sheriff brings him back to the preacher, and we have a wedding on the streets of Oatman right in the middle of Route 66.

ALICE:

My parents, Joe and Aggie, started this restaurant and began serving Mexican food here in 1947. Mom and Dad always cooked, and Dad still is in the kitchen. In 1978 Mom was quite sick and wanted out, so my husband, Stanley, and I talked it over. He's a barber, and barbering had gone way down because at that time everyone was into long hair. Our kids were getting out of high school and needed money for college, so we decided to take it on. We have sent all four of our kids through college out of this restaurant.

Mom is eighty-three and still waitressing two days a week, and our daughter Kimberly came back in 1993 and we turned the restaurant over to her. Dad gets here every morning at eight to cook. So you see, the business is a real generational enterprise.

When Mom and Dad had the café there were always a lot of customers because Route 66 came right through Holbrook. The traffic could be so bad that it was hard to cross the street. In 1979, a year after we took over, the interstate opened, and everything became very quiet, like dead.

Fortunately, Mom and Dad had built up the business with a lot of people from the reservation. They would come to town to do their laundry and get groceries and to sell their crafts, and they always came in here to eat. The Indian people were the only ones that kept up going through that hard period. They saved us. Today they're still coming in.

After Michael Wallis wrote his book, tourists starting coming to Holbrook. Our first big tour was in 1992 when seventy-seven people came from France on a tour of Route 66. We brought in the Native American children to do Indian dances, and they performed right here in the café.

KIMBERLEY GALLEGOS, ALICE GALLEGOS,
AND AGGIE MONTANO, JOE AND AGGIE'S CAFE,
HOLBROOK, ARIZONA

POLLY BROWN

In 1950 Chester E. Lewis built the Wigwam Motel in Holbrook after acquiring the plans from Frank Redford. Redford had designed tepee motel villages made of concrete. A total of seven villages were built throughout the country on the stipulation that Redford be allowed to outfit each room with a pay radio that charged a dime for a half hour of play. His architect's commission was collected each month, in dimes, from these radios.

After the interstate bypassed Holbrook, the Wigwam Village lay dormant for ten years. In 1988 Chester's children, Chester II, Elinor, and John, restored the motel, complete with its original hickory and wicker furniture. They reopened it the following year. Many of their present-day customers once fantasized about staying at the Wigwam when they were kids and have now returned, years later and without their parents, to make fantasy reality.

WIGWAM MOTEL,

HOLBROOK, ARIZONA

POLLY BROWN

MR. D'Z ROUTE 66 DINER,

KINGMAN, ARIZONA

POLLY BROWN

WEST OF OATMAN, ARIZONA

JANE BERNARD

Oatman began as a mining tent camp. It was named in honor of Olive Oatman, who was kidnapped as a young girl by Mojave Indians and later rescued nearby.

Today a small herd of burros comes into town daily from the surrounding mountains. They are all female except for one male who takes care of the entire herd. All the burros have names. When a baby burro is born, the first local to see it has the privilege of naming it. The burros are free to roam as they please and love to mingle with the tourists. Local shops do a brisk business in carrots and feed.

OATMAN, ARIZONA

JANE BERNARD

KINGMAN, ARIZONA

POLLY BROWN

The Museum Club was built in 1931 by taxidermist Dean Eldredge to create a museum and a home for his unique collection, which included stuffed game animals, rifles, and Native American artifacts. The museum was turned into a nightclub in 1936 and today is affectionately known as "The Zoo" because of the collection of animals that still adorns the walls. Car and Driver included the Museum Club in its list of "Top Ten Roadhouses" in the country.

THE MUSEUM CLUB,
FLAGSTAFF, ARIZONA

POLLY BROWN

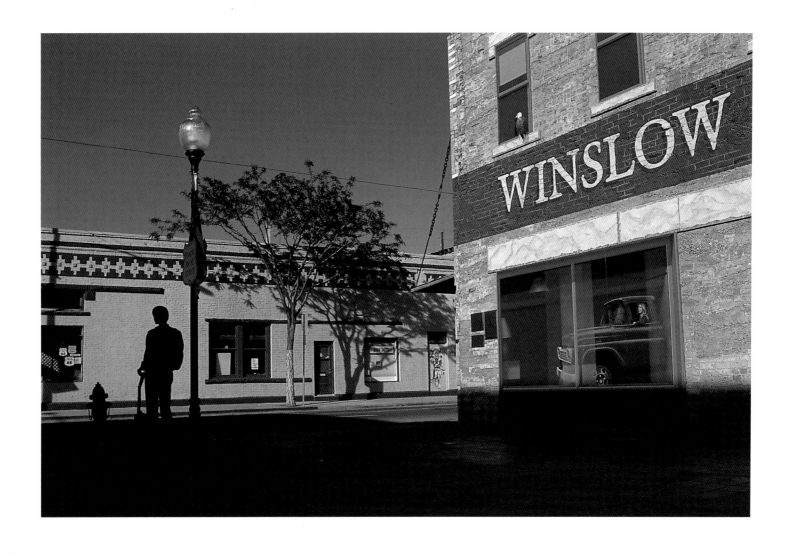

"STANDIN' ON THE CORNER IN WINSLOW,
ARIZONA" PARK

JANE BERNARD

In 1994 the Standin' On the Corner Foundation was formed, dedicated to the rebirth and restoration of historic downtown Winslow. Local business people volunteered to create a park around the theme of the Eagles' famous song "Take It Easy," written by Jackson Browne and Glen Frey. The bronze statue depicts a 1970s-era man standing on the corner wearing jeans and boots with a guitar balanced on the toe of his boot.

EIRIK:

There are eight of us from Norway riding motorcycles from Chicago to Los Angeles. We wanted to make this trip on Route 66 because we had seen a television program that said that it was the first American highway to cross the United States. We were told that we would be able to see the real America by traveling this road.

We planned the trip a year in advance, and we were so excited. We all rented Harley-Davidsons in Chicago because the motorcycles had to be made in America so we could ride the American way.

EIRIK NJARHEIM AND INGE BRIGT AARBAKKE,
ROUTE 66 NORWAY MEN'S TOUR, JACK RABBIT
TRADING POST, JOSEPH CITY, ARIZONA
POLLY BROWN

I have lived on Route 66 all my life. My parents came here from Mexico and my father was a barber. He had a shop one block south of here on the old Route 66. I remember as kids my brothers and sisters would watch for the headlights of the cars at night. We would run out and make our shadows on the buildings from those headlights. That was our TV.

We used to laugh at the Okies during the Dust Bowl years. A family would come through town and have only one mattress strapped to the roof of their car. If they had two, we called them rich Okies. Well, we weren't far from that ourselves. In 1936 we packed up and got ready to go to California. My two older brothers were playing in a local band at that time, and when the band leader found out that he would lose two of his musicians, he pulled some strings and got my brother a job as a laborer on the Santa Fe Railroad. So it was music that kept our family here.

The bypass was very bad for us, but we survived because Seligman was a major terminus for the Santa Fe Railroad. The workers stopped and spent money here, and they supported us. The railroad closed down here in 1986, and on February 18, 1987, I called a meeting to mobilize everyone in Seligman for our economic survival. Only fifteen people showed up because nobody believed we could do anything.

I pushed for the revival of Route 66, and in 1988 it was made an official historic route. So Seligman is the birthplace of the rebirth of Route 66. Today it is better than it ever has been because Seligman is a destination point.

ANGEL DELGADILLO,

ANGEL'S BARBER SHOP,

SELIGMAN, ARIZONA

JANE BERNARD

HACKBERRY GENERAL STORE,

HACKBERRY, ARIZONA

JANE BERNARD

Juan Delgadillo, right, and his son Bob serve up Snow Cap specialties to hungry travelers. The menu lists such choices as "Hamburgers without the Ham," "Cheeseburgers without the Cheese," and "Dead Chicken."

Juan and his father built the place in 1943, and Juan has run it since then with his wife Mary, infusing the business with his special brand of humor. Today their two sons, Bob and John, continue the tradition of providing crumpled napkins and bent straws to customers.

DELGADILLO'S SNOW CAP,
SELIGMAN, ARIZONA

JANE BERNARD

DELGADILLO'S SNOW CAP,

SELIGMAN, ARIZONA

JANE BERNARD

MISS HISTORIC ROUTE 66 BEAUTY QUEEN,

ARIZONA

JANE BERNARD

MISS HISTORIC ROUTE 66 BEAUTY PAGEANT

SELIGMAN, ARIZONA

POLLY BROWN

The two questions we get asked the most often are "Where are the Indians?" and "How can you live out here in the middle of nowhere?"

JERRY HUGHES,
WAITRESS, FRONTIER CAFÉ AND MOTEL,
TRUXTON, ARIZONA

JANE BERNARD

El Rancho

POLLY IS EXCITED about spending the night at the El Rancho Motel in Barstow, California. I am dubious. The woman behind the front desk offers to show us one of the rooms. As we walk up the hill to the room, she says, "Hello, Bob," "Hello, Bob," and "Hello, Bob" to three men who sit outside one of the rooms with half-empty glasses of what appears to be whiskey. Curious.

The woman is a bit out of breath by the time we reach the room. She is quite overweight and probably not used to the climb. The room is small, the furniture shabby, and both the outside door and the bathroom door do not clear the bed. A huge swamp cooler dominates the outside wall, and the place is not particularly clean.

My first instinct is to get in the car and drive away, but I know Polly wants to take some photographs at the hotel, and the woman is standing right there. El Rancho it is.

I am hot, tired, road-weary, and crabby. All I want is to lie down, check my phone messages, and make a few phone calls. Polly disappears with her camera, on the hunt for images.

I pick up the phone only to discover it is black with filth. Filth is somewhat bearable when it is your own, but someone else's filth is another matter. I call the front desk to alert them to the problem, imagining the woman behind the front desk is probably only just beginning to recover from her first hike up to the room. Her son appears at the door a few minutes later with some Windex, and I clean up the phone.

With that taken care of, I lie back down on the bed to make my phone calls and find that I can't seem to get an outside line. This persists for twenty minutes, and I feel my crabbiness increasing. Polly appears at the door, quite cheerful, and says she'll go ask about the phone at the front desk.

California

It turns out the motel only has one outside line and one of the permanent residents is on the phone discussing her Veterans Administration benefits. Somewhere over the course of the next hour we lose the keys to the car. We are unable to unload our bags and our film is baking in the trunk. After a much-frenzied search and a tremendous amount of stress, the keys turn up between the bed and the night table.

We drive out into the desert to photograph evening light and have dinner at the Bagdad Café in Newberry Springs. When we returned to the El Rancho at bedtime, we find that someone — perhaps one of the three Bobs — is listening to Jefferson Airplane. I try to think of it as the El Rancho Lullaby. Sometime in the middle of the night, Polly turns on the swamp cooler because the room is swelteringly hot. It sounds as if a plane is coming in for a landing. Since the swamp cooler is about two inches from Polly's bed, the rest of her night is spent in arctic conditions.

We rise at dawn and wave goodbye to El Rancho.

GORDON:

I am eleven years old. My parents took over managing this motel about a year ago. I help them out, and I have become the minister of the motel. I never was much of a church person, but I just decided that it was time for me to get closer to God. So I started reading the Bible. Then this resident guest, a woman in her nineties, asked me to help her. Since then I have helped other residents in the motel, and I now give weekly services for everyone here.

KEN, CHRISTINE, AND GORDON EVANS,
EL RANCHO MOTEL, BARSTOW, CALIFORNIA
POLLY BROWN

EAST OF BARSTOW, CALIFORNIA

POLLY BROWN

I was just in Sacramento, California. Picked up a general load of freight, and I'm taking it to Hattiesburg, Mississippi. I decided I had some time and I was going to run Old Route 66. I love this highway.

My home in Oklahoma is four miles from Route 66. My wife and I'll take my motorcycle and ride out there to a diner in Weatherford. It's all 1950s and 1960s memorabilia, so we kind of get back in time a little bit and enjoy.

Route 66 is the old highway, and when people travel it they go back to the old way that we were in the 1950s and 1960s. You don't have to turn and look over your shoulder to see who's getting ready to mug you or rob you. It's a chance to get lost in the 1950s, so to speak. You know, people in this country got along with each other a whole lot better then.

RICHARD BRUCE,
TRUCK DRIVER FOR SAVE THE CHILDREN, ON THE
ROAD IN THE MOJAVE DESERT, CALIFORNIA
JANE BERNARD

My dad was a bottle collector for twenty years. He called his hobby "bottles up." He'll be eighty-three next month. Eventually he got tired of it, wrapped the bottles up carefully, and put them all in trash cans and stored them out of sight in his garage.

One weekend I went down to visit him and he had twenty-three boxes of unwrapped bottles on his back porch. I asked him, "What are you going to do with these?" And he said, "Dorothy from the Children's Mental Retardation Center is coming to get them."

I said, "No, she's not," and I loaded them up and left. I didn't even visit. I brought them home and put them out in my garage.

Then my wife got in a bad accident. She had head trauma and they had to airlift her to San Bernardino in a chopper. My mother-in-law came up to live with us and to help take care of her. My wife was a vegetable for a long time, six months.

To take my mind off my troubles, I started building these bottle trees. I've been doing it ever since and I love it. I keep track of them all. I draw them out before I build them. Some of these designs have been drawn a dozen times. It's a twenty-four hour thing with me now. I'm always building or working out here. I'm always dirty, I always need a shower. The whole house can fall down, I don't care. I want to build bottle trees.

A few people have asked me to build them bottle trees and I won't do it. This isn't about money; it's about a love for what I'm doing. Plus, I'm too busy to do it for someone else. Someone wants to build a bottle tree? Hey, I've got a welding machine, I've got the materials. Let them come do it, but I ain't got time.

ELMER LONG,

BOTTLE TREE ARTIST, OLD ROUTE 66,

BETWEEN VICTORVILLE AND BARSTOW, CALIFORNIA

POLLY BROWN

I've seen a lot of famous people come through here over the years. Pearl Bailey was a personal favorite of mine. Elvis only came in here one time. I started to wait on him, but he stopped to look at the jukebox first. He didn't see any of his records on there. I don't know why because we always had them on there, but I think the Beatles were very popular then. He got mad and just walked out the door.

HILDA FISH,
WAITRESS, THE SUMMIT INN, CAJON PASS,
OAK HILLS, CALIFORNIA
POLLY BROWN

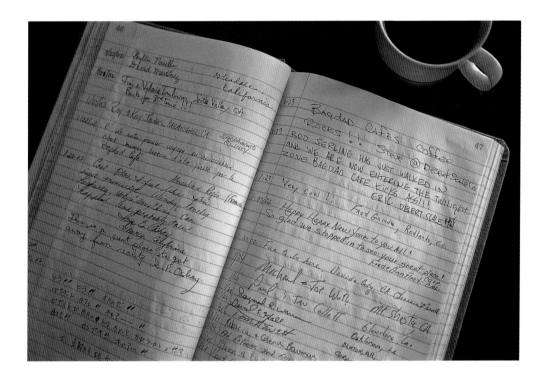

BAGDAD CAFÉ, NEWBERRY SPRINGS,

CALIFORNIA

JANE BERNARD

Entries in the guest book at the Bagdad
Café speak to the cult status of the restaurant and the movie by the same name.

LINDA HILL,
WAITRESS, LUDLOW CAFÉ,
LUDLOW, CALIFORNIA
JANE BERNARD

ROBERT ERWIN,

GOFF'S GENERAL STORE, ESSEX, CALIFORNIA

POLLY BROWN

I worked as a teacher in Los Angeles and wanted to get away from all that. I didn't buy the place looking for no capital gains. In fact, my wife thought I was kind of stupid, and so did the bank. I would go to the bank to make a loan, and they'd say, "You want to make a loan to do what? Where? Get outta here"! I was just interested in the store. The funny thing is I never knew I was located on the Mother road until people started coming around and taking pictures of the building.

Opened in 1976, the museum houses the memories and personal treasures of Roy and Dale. Roy's beloved horse, Trigger; Dale's horse, Buttermilk; and their loyal dog, Bullet, are stuffed and on display. A documentary about their life together runs hourly, and it brought us to tears. It quotes Roy as saying to Dale, "When I go, I want you to stuff me and put me up there on Trigger." The museum is scheduled to relocate to Branson, Missouri, in 2003.

THE ROY ROGERS–DALE EVANS MUSEUM, VICTORVILLE, CALIFORNIA

POLLY BROWN

DIXIE EVANS,

EXOTIC WORLD BURLESQUE MUSEUM,

HELENDALE, CALIFORNIA

JANE BERNARD

The purpose of the museum is to educate the public about burlesque. Our displays start with the 1920s, because burlesque was very popular then, and continue through the 1930s, 1940s, and 1950s. We have Sally Rand's original fans, Gypsy Rose Lee's costumes and trunks, Jayne Mansfield's ottoman, and the hat that Marilyn Monroe wore in *Some Like it Hot*. We have ten or twelve glass counters full of bracelets, rings, jewelry, pasties, net bras, G-strings, and lots of small articles that were parts of costumes. Then, of course, we have gowns and dresses

and promotional pictures of many of the performers. Little by little, girls have donated their costumes and photos. Someone mailed me this photo of Lili St. Cyr with Eleanor Roosevelt.

Before burlesque theaters there was no affordable entertainment for working-class people. You see, burlesque is comedy. It mimics and exaggerates what is real. It's not just a bunch of strippers, no! It's a big show! They had comedians and they had pretty girls and a chorus line and entertainers and different acts. Times were tough then, and for the price of a loaf of bread people could fall into one of these burlesque theaters and everything was up, up, laughing, funny, silly stories, beautiful girls, songs and dancers, and no stage waits. The audience could escape reality for two and a half hours.

I started performing in 1941 in USO shows in the Long Beach area. I was offered a job as a page in a theater in San Francisco and I thought, "Oh, this is going to be a wonderful career! I'm going to get $55 a week for the rest of my life and I can acquire some clothes!" Well, the show went broke in two weeks, and I had no money to get home to Los Angeles.

I wandered down the block to this striptease nightclub, and there was Sondra Corrina performing. She had a big white cowboy hat on and fur chaps and she was shooting these fake guns off and bumping and grinding. The place was filled with redheads and blondes and they all looked so glamorous. A fellow came up and punched me in the arm and said, "I want you to cut your act short and get out and mix a little more." I said, "I don't work here," and he said, "Do you want to?"

The rent was due and I had no money, so I went to see the boss and he told me, "I'll pay you $75 a week and you'll make another $25 on commissions and tips."

Well, the girls were the sweetest girls I've ever met in my whole life. One day my boss yanked me into his office and said, "You don't belong here. Do you know they have big burlesque theaters back east?" He put me in touch with an agent and off I went.

I started out at $350 a week. I had a whole Hollywood number. I'd come on stage in dark glasses with a long cigarette holder and sing, "You Are My Lucky Star." Oh, I'd really flaunt it all over the stage. The curtains would open behind me and I'd walk onto my set. There was a beautiful red velvet couch and a producer's chair on one side and a big movie camera on the other. The band would play, "You Ought to Be in Pictures" and I'd say, "Who, me?" and they'd yell, "Yes, you!" Then I'd stroll over to the camera and the lights would go off and on and off and on and I'd take a screen test and then I'd take some wardrobe off. And then I'd walk over to the producer's chair, very confident, like I had the part, and when I found out I didn't, I would rock and yell and scream and cry and throw myself on the stage and throw a violent tantrum.

Then I'd crawl all the way across to the producer's chair and the band would play "Just One More Chance." Then I'd say, "Oh, you and me on the couch? Oh, my gosh!" and I'd stroll

over to the couch while the band would play a real low-down blues number, and I'd bump and grind and mimic a sex act and take off everything. Then, of course, I'd go over to the producer's chair and sign a big movie contract.

I went back east with that act and my boss, Mr. Minsky, said, "You look like Marilyn Monroe when you come on stage," and I said, "Mr. Minsky, everyone in Hollywood looks like Marilyn." He replied, "Well, I'm going to call you the Marilyn Monroe of burlesque." So then I had to act and talk like her, and when I took everything off, I did it just like Marilyn. So if you couldn't ever see the real Marilyn, you could come to the burlesque and see me. Oh golly, gee, I might have shown you more than Marilyn, too.

She tried to sue me, too, but she lost. My act was kind of raunchy, but I was not making fun of Marilyn. I was just doing a wild, sexy strip act. I wasn't aware of how fragile she was. Of course, after she died the shock was absolutely horrendous. It was only after it was all over that we realized Marilyn actually had very little.

When she died, I went into a horrible depression. I was living in New York at the time. It was terrible. I felt such guilt. I didn't care if I worked again. I didn't care about anything, and I drank an awful lot and stayed drunk for a couple of years. Then I ran into an old friend on the street, and when she heard I wasn't working, she asked me if I wanted to open for her. She had no idea what bad shape I was in.

So I called my Christian Science practitioner, Doddie Goodman, and she said, "Dixie, if you were Marilyn, would you want to be remembered or would you want to be forgotten?" I had to admit I would want to be remembered. So she said, "You do Marilyn and you do her good. Don't you do one vulgar moment or motion. You do a portrait of her and you do it right." Then she said, "Do you want to live in a palace or live in a garbage can? You put down the drinks and don't drink anymore."

So I stopped drinking right then and there and created a portrait of Marilyn. The theater was on the Upper East Side and very elegant. I did little bits from every one of her movies.

Toward the end of my act, I would say, "I've got a right to sing the blues," and the band would play that song. Then I'd hold up my hand, which had a big, big fake diamond on it, and I would say, "You've brought me so much and so little," and then I'd drink a lot of champagne and the band would play "The Blue Prelude," and then I'd take the glass, put a pill in it, drink it, and scream. The lights would go out, and when they came back up, I'd roll in my furs and say, "But this is how I want you to remember me. A kiss on the hand may be quite continental..." and I would walk off with the band playing that number.

When I walked through the crowd, I couldn't believe it. I got a standing ovation! Yes, they were all crying and saying, "Thank you for bringing Marilyn back."

I came to the United States in 1983, and I first saw this place in 1989. Since then, this has been my dream, but I really don't know why. I have other hotels, and I was finally able to lease this place in 1999. We repainted the tepees and are slowly fixing the place up.

SURESH PATEL,
WIGWAM MOTEL, RIALTO, CALIFORNIA

JANE BERNARD

WIGWAM MOTEL,

RIALTO, CALIFORNIA

JANE BERNARD

REST STOP,
MOJAVE DESERT, CALIFORNIA

POLLY BROWN

PACIFIC PARK,

SANTA MONICA PIER, CALIFORNIA

JANE BERNARD

SANTA MONICA PIER,

SANTA MONICA, CALIFORNIA

POLLY BROWN

Appendix of Businesses Operating on Route 66

ILLINOIS:

25 LOU MITCHELL'S RESTAURANT AND BAKERY
565 West Jackson
Chicago, IL 60661
312-939-3111

23 WILLOWBROOK BALLROOM
8900 South Archer Avenue
Willow Springs, IL 60480
708-839-1000
www.willowbrookballroom.com

DELL RHEA'S CHICKEN BASKET
645 Joliet Road
Old Route 66
Willowbrook, IL 60521
630-325-0780
www.chickson66@route66.com

37 JOHN WEISS
Route 66 Association of Illinois
P.O. Box 16
Frankfort, IL 60423
KAYO66@aol.com

28 POLK-A-DOT DRIVE INN
222 North Front Street
Braidwood, IL 60408
815-458-3377

21 RIVIERA RESTAURANT
5650 East Route #53
Gardner, IL 60424
815-237-2344

OLD LOG CABIN RESTAURANT
Old Route 66 North and Aurora Street
Pontiac, IL 61764
815-842-2908
www.oldlogcabin.com

31 RUBY'S CHAIR CANING
610 John Street
Pontiac, IL 61764
815-844-5575

34 FUNK'S GROVE MAPLE SIRUP
RR 1, Box 41A
Shirley, IL 61772
309-874-3360
www.route66.com/FunksGrove/

DIXIE TRUCKER'S HOME
Route 136 and I-55
Exit 145
McLean, IL 61754
309-874-2323

SHEA'S HISTORIC ROUTE 66 MUSEUM
2075 Peoria Road
Springfield, IL 62702
217-522-0475

THE COZY DOG DRIVE-IN
2935 South Sixth Street
Springfield, IL 62703
217-525-1992
www.cozydogdrivein.com

MOTHER JONES MONUMENT
2/10 of a mile from Highway 66
Located in the Union Miners' Cemetery
Mount Olive, IL 62069

OUR LADY OF THE HIGHWAY SHRINE
Raymond, IL 62560

26 HENRY'S OLD ROUTE 66 RABBIT RANCH
"Home of Snortin' Norton"
Old Route 66 and Madison
Staunton, IL 62088-2127
618-635-5655
route66@midwest.net

MUSTANG CORRAL
5446 Chain of Rocks Road
Edwardsville, IL 62025
800-327-2897

MISSOURI:

TED DREW'S FROZEN CUSTARD
6726 Chippewa Street
St Louis, MO 63109
314-481-2652

41 MOLLY'S
816 Geyer Avenue
St. Louis, MO
314-436-0921

168

44 RED CEDAR INN
1047 East Osage
Pacific, MO 63069
636-257-9790
www.home.att.net/~red.cedar.inn

MERAMEC CAVERNS
I-44
West Stanton, MO
573-468-3166
www.americascave.com

51 ROUTE 66 LOUNGE
Old Highway 66
1205 Washington
Cuba, MO 65453
573-885-3007

WAGON WHEEL MOTEL
901 East Washington
(I-44, exit 208)
Cuba, MO 65453
573-885-3411

52 GRANNY'S BIRD HOUSE
11020 Dillon Outer Road
Rolla, MO 65401
573-364-6435
gold1200@hotmail.com

ONYX MOUNTAIN CAVERNS
14705 PD 8541
Between Waynesville and Rolla on I-44
Newburg, MO 65550
573-762-3341

MUNGER MOSS MOTEL
1336 East Route 66
Lebanon, MO 65536
417-532-3111
www.route66.com/mungermoss/index

40 WRINK'S MARKET
Route 5, Box 427
Lebanon, MO 65536
417-532-3201

54 ENCHANTED VALLEY INTERSKATE
P.O. Box 2017
Lebanon, MO 65536
417-532-5701
e-mail: interskate@webound.com

42 EXOTIC ANIMAL PARADISE
124 Jungle Drive
Strafford, MO 65757
1-888-570-9898
www.exoticanimalparadise.com

ROLLER CITY
2664 East Kearney Street
Springfield, MO 65803
417-864-7388
www.rollercity.com

49 66 DRIVE-IN THEATER
17231 Old 66 Boulevard
Carthage, MO 64836-9206
417-359-5959
www.ComeVisit.com/66drivein/

48 BOOTS MOTEL
107 South Garrison
Carthage, MO 64836
417-358-9453

39 PRECIOUS MOMENTS CHAPEL
4321 Chapel Road
Carthage, MO 64836
800-543-7957
www.preciousmoments.com

KANSAS:

61 EISLER BROTHERS' OLD RIVERTON STORE
On Historic 66
Riverton, KS 66770
620-848-3330

CAFÉ ON THE ROUTE
1101 Military Avenue
Baxter Springs, KS 66713
316-856-5646

OKLAHOMA:

66 Y CLUB
616 North Mickey Mantle
Commerce, OK 74339
918-675-5414

69 COLEMAN THEATER
103 North Main Street
Miami, OK 74354
918-540-2425

WAYLAN'S KU-KU BURGER
915 North Main
Miami, OK 74354
918-542-1524

65 THE FIDDLE HOUSE AND TOTEM POLE PARK
4 miles east of Foyil on 28A
Foyil, OK 74354
918-342-9149

THE TOP HAT DAIRY BAR
On Route 66 and 28A
Foyil, OK 74354
918-341-0477

74 THE BLUE WHALE
Catoosa, OK 74015

78 METRO DINER
3001 East Eleventh Street
Tulsa, OK 74104
918-592-2616

79 P. J.'S BAR-B-QUE
1423 Manuel
Chandler, OK 74834
405-258-1167

MUSEUM OF PIONEER HISTORY
717 Manvel
Chandler, OK 74834
405-258-2425

THE LINCOLN MOTEL
740 East First Street
Chandler, OK 74834
405-258-0200

71 THE OLD ROUND BARN
P.O. Box 134
Arcadia, OK 73007
405-396-2761
www.digitalmonkey.com/oldbarn

OKLAHOMA CITY NATIONAL MEMORIAL
P.O. Box 323
Oklahoma City, OK 73101
405-235-3313

66 BOWL
3810 NW Thirty-Ninth Street
Oklahoma City, OK 73112
405-946-2717
www.okclive.com

JOB'S DRIVE-IN
1220 Sunset Drive
El Reno, OK 73039
405-262-0194

FLASHBACK MEMORABILIA
P.O. Box 1504
Clinton, OK 73601
1-800-309-6120
www.flashbackmemorabilia.com

67 BILL'S BARBER SHOP
704 Frisco
Clinton, OK 73601

OKLAHOMA ROUTE 66 MUSEUM
2229 Gary Boulevard
Clinton, OK 73601-5304
580-323-7866
www.route66.org

OLD TOWN MUSEUM
Corner of Highway 66 and Pioneer Road
P.O. Box 542
Elk City, OK 73648

NATIONAL ROUTE 66 MUSEUM
2701 West Third Street
Old Route 66
Elk City, OK 73648
580-225-2207

SAND HILLS CURIOSITY SHOP
P.O. Box 121
201 South Sheb Wooley Avenue
Erick, OK 73645
580-526-3738

TEXAS:
JONES HONEY AND BEE APIARY
Route 2, Box 53
Lela, TX 79079
806-246-2605

CACTUS INN
Route 66 West
McLean, TX 79057
806-779-2346

DEVIL'S ROPE MUSEUM
Old Route 66 and 100 Kingsley Street
McLean, TX 79057
806-779-2225
www.barbwiremuseum.com

RED RIVER STEAK HOUSE
Old Route 66
McLean, TX 79057-0289
806-779-8940

THE WORLD'S LARGEST CROSS
Cross Ministries
Groom, TX 79039
806-248-9006

INDIAN MOTORCYCLE
6400 I-40 West
Amarillo, TX 79106
806-463-7727

89
95 THE BIG TEXAN STEAK RANCH
7701 I-40 East
Amarillo, TX 79120-7000
800-657-7177
www.bigtexan.com

VICTORIANA ANTIQUE STORE
3300-3302 Sixth Street
Amarillo, TX 79106
806-374-6568

85 DOT'S MINI MUSEUM
105 North Twelfth Street
Vega, TX 79092
806-267-2367

84 MIDPOINT CAFÉ
Route 66 (I-40, Exit 22)
Adrian, TX 79001
866-538-6380
www.midpoint66.com

NEW MEXICO:

101 TEE PEE CURIOS
924 East Tucumcari Boulevard
Tucumcari, NM 88401
505-461-3773
callens@plateautel.net

122 THE BLUE SWALLOW MOTEL
815 East Tucumcari Boulevard
Tucumcari, NM 88401
505-461-9849
www.blueswallow.com

ROUTE 66 AUTO MUSEUM
2766 Old Route 66
Santa Rosa, NM 88435
505-472-1966
www.rt66automuseum.com

117 BOZO'S GARAGE AND WRECKER SERVICE
2601 Will Rogers Drive
Santa Rosa, NM 88435
505-472-3368

JOSEPH'S RESTAURANT
865 Old Route 66
Santa Rosa, NM 88435
505-472-3361
www.route66.com/josephs

LAKE CITY DINER
101 Fourth Street
Santa Rosa, NM 88435
505-472-5253

SUNSET MOTEL
929 Will Rogers Drive
Santa Rosa, NM 88435
505-472-3762

110 CHIEF'S AUTO PARTS
Santa Rosa, NM 88435
505-472-3227

FLYING STAR CAFÉ
3416 Central Avenue, SE
Albuquerque, NM 87106
505-255-6633

112 LARRY'S HATS
3102 Central Avenue, SE
Albuquerque, NM 87106
505-266-2095

97 AZTEC MOTEL
3821 Central Avenue, NE
Albuquerque, NM 87108
505-255-4889

108 ROUTE 66 DINER
14405 Central Avenue, NE
Albuquerque, NM 87108
505-247-1421
www.66diner.com

AMERICAN WOMAN, INC.
Tattoos, Nails, Tanning, Permanent
Cosmetics, and Piercing
5309 Silver, SE
Albuquerque, NM 87108
505-255-1026

URANIUM CAFÉ
519 West Santa Fe Avenue
Grants, NM 87020
505-287-7540

118 SWAP MEET 66
8500 Highway 66
Bluewater, NM 87005
505-876-4989

THE NAVAJO CO-OP
P.O. Box 838
Thoreau, NM 87323
505-862-8075
www.navajo-coop.org

105 EARL'S FAMILY RESTAURANT
1400 East 66 Avenue
Gallup, NM 87301
505-863-4201

116 THE RANCH KITCHEN
119 3001 West Highway 66
Gallup, NM 87301
505-722-2537
rkitchen@cia-g.com

EL RANCHO HOTEL AND MOTEL
I-40, Exit 22
1000 East Sixty-Sixth Avenue
Gallup, NM 87301
800-543-6351
www.elranchohotel.com

106 RICHARDSON'S TRADING POST
222 West Highway 66
Gallup, NM 87301
505-722-4762
www.richardsontrading.com

ARIZONA:

127 STEWART'S PETRIFIED WOOD
128 15 miles east of Holbrook
Adamana, AZ
800-414-8533
www.petrifiedwood.com

131 JOE AND AGGIE'S CAFÉ
120 West Hopi Drive
Holbrook, AZ 86025
888-266-8078

132 WIGWAM MOTEL
811 West Hopi Drive
Holbrook, AZ 86025
928-524-3048

139 JACK RABBIT TRADING POST
Joseph City, AZ
928-288-3230

LA POSADA HOTEL
303 East Second Street
Winslow, AZ 86047
928-289-4366
www.laposada.org

138 "STANDIN' ON THE CORNER IN WINSLOW, ARIZONA" PARK
www.standinonthecorner.com

137 THE MUSEUM CLUB
3404 East Route 66
Flagstaff, AZ 86004
928-526-9434
www.museumclub.com

129 WINTER SUN TRADING COMPANY
107 North San Francisco Street
Suite #1
Flagstaff, AZ 86001
928-774-2884
www.wintersun.com

MACY'S COFFEE HOUSE
14 South Beaver Street
Flagstaff, AZ 86001
928-774-2243
www.macyscoffee.com

142 DELGADILLO'S SNOW CAP
143 Old Route 66
Seligman, AZ 86337
Rdelgad475@aol.com
928-422-3291

140 ANGEL'S BARBER SHOP
ANGEL AND VILMA DELGADILLO'S MEMORABILIA
217 East Route 66
Seligman, AZ 86337
928-422-3352
www.route66giftshop.com

GRAND CANYON CAVERNS
P.O. Box 180
Peach Springs, AZ 86434
928-422-3223
www.gccaverns.com

147 FRONTIER CAFÉ AND MOTEL
HC 35, Box 31
Peach Springs, AZ 86434
928-769-2238

141 HACKBERRY GENERAL STORE
Hackberry, AZ
928-769-2605

POWERHOUSE VISITOR CENTER
333 West Andy Devine Avenue
Kingman, AZ 86401
928-753-6106

133 MR. D'Z ROUTE 66 DINER
105 East Andy Devine Avenue
Kingman, AZ 86401
928-718-0066

OATMAN CHAMBER OF COMMERCE
P.O. Box 423
Oatman, AZ, 86433
928-768-6222
www.oatmangoldroad.com

CALIFORNIA:

HIGH SAHARA OASIS
31251 Goff's Road
Essex, CA 92332
760-733-4032

156 GOFF'S GENERAL STORE
119246 Goff's Road
Essex, CA 92332
760-733-9918

154 BAGDAD CAFÉ
46548 National Trails Highway
Newberry Springs, CA 92365
760-257-3101
www.lppublishing.com/bagdadcafe.html

155 LUDLOW CAFÉ
Ludlow, CA
760-733-4501

149 EL RANCHO MOTEL
112 East Main Street
Old Route 66
Barstow, CA 92311
760-256-2401

158 EXOTIC WORLD BURLESQUE MUSEUM
29053 Wild Road
Helendale, CA 92342
760-243-5261
www.exoticworldusa.org

153 THE SUMMIT INN
Top of Cajon Pass
6000 Mariposa Road-15
Oak Hills, CA 92345
760-949-1313

161
162 WIGWAM MOTEL
2728 West Foothill Boulevard
Rialto, CA 92376
909-875-3005